SUTTON POCKET HISTORIES

ANCIENT EGYPT

BARBARA WATTERSON

SUTTON PUBLISHING

First published in the United Kingdom in 1998 by
Sutton Publishing Limited · Phoenix Mill
Thrupp · Stroud · Gloucestershire · GL5 2BU

British Library Cataloguing in Publication Data
A catalogue record for this book is available from the British
Library.

ISBN 0-7509-0802-5

Cover picture: Scarab Pectoral, from the tomb of Tutankhamun,
in the Valley of the Kings at Thebes (Egyptian National
Museum/photograph: Giraudon/Bridgeman Art Library,
London).

 ALAN SUTTON™ and SUTTON™ are the
trade marks of Sutton Publishing Limited

Typeset in 11/16 pt Baskerville.
Typesetting and origination by
Sutton Publishing Limited.
Printed in Great Britain by
The Guernsey Press Company Limited,
Guernsey Channel Islands.

*For Juan, Juana and Paul
but above all for Alice*

BOOKS BY THE SAME AUTHOR

Contents

Preface

1998 marks not only twenty years of history publishing at Sutton but is also the bicentennial year of Napoleon's Expedition to Egypt. When Napoleon landed in Alexandria on 1 July 1798 his aim was not only to use Egypt as a stepping stone to India, but also to bring enlightenment to the country after nearly 300 years of Ottoman rule. To this end he took with him 175 'learned civilians' and his expedition, though ill advised militarily, was, thanks to them, of inestimable value from an archaeological standpoint, for it set in motion the scientific study of ancient Egypt, Egyptology. By 1822 Jean François Champollion (1790–1832) had deciphered hieroglyphs; and in 1858, Auguste Mariette (1821–81) founded the Egyptian Antiquities Service, putting a stop to the wholesale plunder and unrestrained sale of Egyptian antiquities that had devastated archaeological sites. Between them, Champollion and Mariette opened the way for the great philological achievements and scientific excavations of the last century or so, enabling us to achieve a greater understanding of the history and culture of one of the world's greatest civilizations.

List of Dates

Egyptologists arrange ancient Egyptian history into dynasties of kings, following the system invented by Manetho, a scholar-priest who lived in the third century BC, probably in the temple at Sebennytos in the Nile Delta. Hence the historic era in Egypt is called the Dynastic Period. The prehistoric period, dating to the time before the unification of the country under one ruler, is termed Predynastic. Manetho's original list of dynasties has been supplemented by two more to cover the years after his death, so that whereas his list ended in 343 BC, the modern list ends with the coming of Alexander the Great in 332 BC. The thirty-two dynasties thus arrived at are subdivided into three groups under headings called 'kingdoms', a term that in this context means a unified state and is not a reference to geographical boundaries. The periods when there was no strong central government are known as 'intermediate periods'.

Predynastic Period
in Lower Egypt (i.e. the Faiyum) from *c.* 5200 BC
in Upper Egypt from *c.* 4300 BC

Archaic Period, *c.* 3100–*c.* 2686 BC
Dynasty I, *c.* 3100–*c.* 2890
Dynasty II, *c.* 2890–*c.* 2686

Old Kingdom, *c.* 2686–*c.* 2181 BC
Dynasty III, *c.* 2686–*c.* 2613
Dynasty IV, *c.* 2613–*c.* 2494
Dynasty V, *c.* 2494–*c.* 2345
Dynasty VI, *c.* 2345–*c.* 2181

First Intermediate Period, *c.* 2181–c. 2040 BC
Dynasty VII, *c.* 2181–*c.* 2173
Dynasty VIII, *c.* 2173–*c.* 2160
Dynasty IX, *c.* 2160–*c.* 2130
Dynasty X, *c.* 2130–*c.* 2040

Middle Kingdom, *c.* 2106–1633(?) BC
Dynasty XI, *c.* 2106—1963
Dynasty XII, 1963–1786
Dynasty XIII, 1786–1633(?)

Second Intermediate Period, 1786–1550 BC
Dynasty XIV, 1786–*c.* 1603
Dynasty XV, 1648–1540

LIST OF DATES

Dynasty XVI, *c.* 1648–1587
Dynasty XVII, *c.* 1648–1550

New Kingdom, 1550–1070/69 BC
Dynasty XVIII, 1550–1295
Dynasty XIX, 1295–1186
Dynasty XX, 1186–1070/69

Third Intermediate Period, 1070/69–525 BC
Dynasty XXI (at Tanis), 1070/69–945
Dynasty XXI (at Thebes), 1080–945
Dynasty XXII, 945–715
Dynasty XXIII, 818–715
Dynasty XXIV, 728–715
Dynasty XXV (Kushite), 716–664
Dynasty XXVI (Saite), 664–525

The Late Period, 525–332 BC
Dynasty XXVII (Persian), 525–404
Dynasty XXVIII, 404–399
Dynasty XXIX, 399–380
Dynasty XXX, 380–343
Dynasty XXXI (Persian), 343–332

Alexander the Great, 332–323 BC

Manetho wrote in Greek, hence it became the custom among early Egyptologists to refer to Egyptian kings by the names used by Manetho, a convention reinforced by the fact that we do not know with any degree of certainty how ancient Egyptian was pronounced. Today, however, it is becoming the custom to give the kings their Egyptian names; hence those formerly known, for example, as Cheops, Chephren, Mycerinus, Sesostris, Amenemmes or Tuthmosis are now called Khufu, Khafre, Menkaure, Senwosret, Amenemhat and Thutmose.

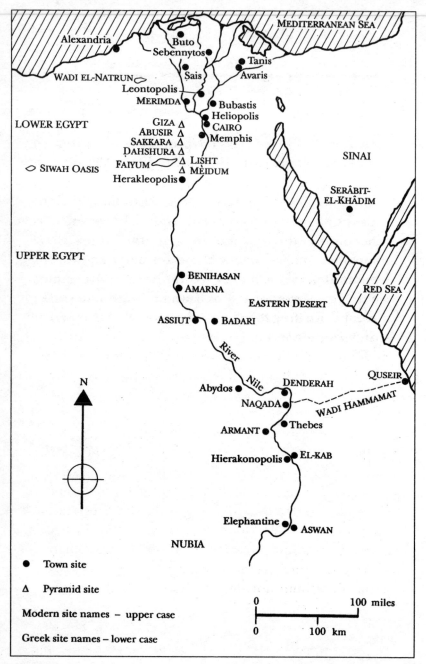

Map of Egypt.

Introduction: Landscape and Resources

Egypt is a land that might never have come into existence. Some sixty million years ago a large area of north Africa, including the north-eastern corner where Egypt is situated, was covered by the waters of a sea known to geologists today as the Tethys, the forerunner of the Mediterranean. Over many millennia, the Tethys enlarged and contracted, but about thirty million years ago it receded from Africa for the last time and the Mediterranean coast assumed roughly the shape it has now.

Five million or so years before the Tethys underwent its final contraction, a geological event that was to shape the nature of the land of Egypt occurred in the mountain regions of Ethiopia and Uganda. Two streams, the Blue Nile and the White Nile, began to flow northwards towards the Tethys, converging at Khartoum in the Sudan and from there flowing as a single river for some 3,000 km to the sea. From Khartoum northwards the flow of the Nile is interrupted by a series of rapids or cataracts. The Sixth Cataract is just downstream from Khartoum; the First, which is nearly 1,800 km to the north at Aswan, marks the river's entry into the Nile Valley.

The Nile was once immensely wide, bordered by marshland and swamps, but over the millennia the river narrowed; the different stages in the level of its bed can now be seen in the form of cliffs and terraces on the east and west sides of the Nile Valley. It flowed through land that sloped gently from south to north – today Aswan is 113 m above sea level, Luxor 79 m and Cairo 37 m – with the result that gradually detritus accumulated at its mouth to form a delta. The river flooded its banks in an annual Inundation, which took place between July and October and covered most of the Nile Valley and the Delta. As the flood waters receded, a layer of fertile silt was deposited over the land. This deposition is thought to have begun about 8000 BC, and for nearly ten thousand years silt accumulated at the rate of about 7½ cm a century to reach an average depth of 9 m. All of Egypt's cultivable land owed its existence to the Nile and its actions, giving rise to Herodotus' observation that Egypt was 'the gift of the river'.

When the Tethys receded from Egypt, the skeletons of marine animals that had once lived in it hardened into a thick chalky layer of sedimentary rock – limestone. These marine animals were, in the main, a type of *foraminifera* which, because of their coin-shaped shells, have been given the name nummulites (from the Latin *nummus*, coin); and the surface of Egypt, from the Mediterranean in the north almost to the southern border at Aswan, is largely made up of nummulitic limestone. At Aswan the limestone layer has been removed by erosion to reveal granite and dolerite, the igneous rocks of the old continent. Between Aswan and Gebel Silsileh, some 63 km to the north, the rock is sandstone.

About forty million years ago Arabia split away from the African continent of which it had previously been a part. The split took place along the Red Sea, which continues to widen and is part of the great rift system which extends from the Dead Sea to East Africa. For the whole of its length the rift depression is balanced by uplift along its borders. In eastern Egypt this uplift has resulted in mountains up to 2,000 m high which border the Red Sea and in which the old continental rocks have been exposed by erosion of the overlying layers of limestone and sandstone.

Modern Egypt has an area of about 1,002,000 sq km, much of which is desert. The inhabitable and cultivable part of the land, that is, the area consisting of the Delta and the Nile Valley, the Faiyum depression and the oases in the Western Desert, measures only about 36,000 sq km and was undoubtedly less in ancient times. It is composed of two distinct portions: the broad Delta and a small part of the valley to its south; and the narrow Nile Valley proper. The former is called Lower Egypt, the latter Upper Egypt; and there are marked geographical dissimilarites between the Two Lands, as the ancient Egyptians called them, with a tendency on the part of their inhabitants to think of themselves as separate peoples.

RESOURCES

Egypt's principal resources were a seemingly inexhaustible supply of Nile water and alluvium, the basis of its agriculture, and stone, available in quantity and variety for building and artistic purposes. The rift mountains of the Eastern Desert were rich in gold and for centuries mines at Coptos were worked. As these became exhausted or too difficult, mining activity was transferred to Lower Nubia. Copper was obtained from the Sinai Peninsula and Lower Nubia, and copper, tin and lead from the Red Sea area of the Eastern Desert. Lead was mined at Aswan, but the iron deposits there were ignored and the comparatively rare meteoritic iron, obtained from meteorites that had fallen in the desert, was the only iron known to the Egyptians until the telluric metal was imported from the Near East from about 1000 BC. The Red Sea area produced emerald, Egypt's only precious stone; and beryl, feldspar, jasper and porphyry. Amethyst and steatite were found near Aswan; and malachite in the Eastern Desert, Lower Nubia and the Sinai Peninsula, which was also a source of turquoise. Alum, gypsum and, above all, natron, the carbonate of soda vital to the practice of mummification, were found in the Western Desert.

Palm trees grew in abundance: dom palm (*Hyphaene thebaica*), from whose nuts a drink was made; and date palm (*Phoenix dactylifer*). The date palm needs artificial pollination, and hand-pollination seems to have been practised from early dynastic times. Palm wood was commonly used for roofing, but otherwise the quality of Egypt's timber was poor and largely useless for building or artistic purposes. The country was deficient in wood, though trees were probably not so scarce in pharaonic times as they are now. Indigenous trees included the Egyptian willow (*Salis subserrta*), tamarisk (*Tamarisk nilotica*), and two oil-producing trees, moringa (*Moringa peregrina*) and acacia (*Acacia nilotica*). The sycamore fig tree (*Ficus sycomorus*)[1] was not native to Egypt, but was cultivated at least from the First Dynasty, as were vines for the production of wine.

What Egypt lacked in trees was compensated for by the plant *Cyperus papyrus* which, in ancient times, grew in abundance in the marshes of the Nile Valley and the Delta, although it no longer does so. Almost every part of the papyrus plant was utilized to make ropes, mats, boxes, sandals and even boats. Above all, the stalk, sliced into thin sections that were laid side by side and crosswise, then pressed into sheets and dried in the sun, formed an unsurpassed writing material.

The terrain of the upland areas to the west of the Nile Valley and in the northern Red Sea hills was less arid than it is now and supported large numbers of rhinoceros, elephant, giraffe, deer, ibex, antelope, gazelle, wild ass and cattle and ostrich, which the Egyptians hunted. The two main food crops grown by ancient Egyptians were barley (*Hordeum vulgare*) and emmer wheat (*Triticum dicoccum*). Yeast (*Saccharomyes winlocki*) was used for fermentation. Pulses, especially beans and lentils, onions, garlic, lettuce, celery and herbs, such as fenugreek, thyme, marjoram, liquorice and mint, were widely grown. In addition, there were many varieties of edible fish in the Nile, although there were also crocodiles and hippopotami.

ONE

The Earliest Egyptians

The end of the last Ice Age in Europe (about 10,000 BC) caused north Africa to become hotter and more dessicated, and therefore less hospitable to the nomads who lived there. Attracted by favourable conditions in the Faiyum depression in the Western Desert, they settled there and developed from nomadic hunters into sedentary agriculturalists. By about 5200 BC their diet was still supplemented by hunting, but they were cultivating emmer wheat, six-rowed barley and flax, which was spun on a spindle to produce a thread from which was woven coarse linen for use as clothing. The oldest-known predynastic site in the northern Nile Valley is Merimda, on the western edge of the Delta some 90 km north of the Faiyum. It was first settled in about 5000 BC, some seven hundred years earlier than the earliest-known settlement in Upper Egypt.

The oldest predynastic culture in southern Egypt was the Badarian, which flourished between 4300 and 3800 BC. It gave rise to a higher standard of living and an increased use of metal. The later culture, dating to about 4000 BC, originated in the region of modern Luxor and is known as Naqada I. Its influence gradually became more widely spread, so that from about 3500 BC a distinctive culture, known as Naqada II, had emerged. During the Naqada II period so many technological and cultural advances were made that it is now seen as the precursor of ancient Egyptian civilization.

The predynastic cultures of Upper Egypt lived in settlements which, by the Naqada II period, had become walled towns with houses made of mud brick. All inhabitants practised agriculture and had a knowlegde of copper and produced excellent hand-made pottery. The predynastic cultures of Lower Egypt were different: they do not seem to have made the same progress as those of Upper Egypt, perhaps because, living in an area that was agriculturally more prolific than Upper Egypt, they lacked incentive. All the predynastic cultures clearly had a belief in some form of afterlife and made provision for it in their graves.

From about 3250 BC Upper Egypt entered a transitional era, the Protodynastic or Naqada III. During this period, which lasted about 150 years, certain centres of predynastic culture, especially Naqada, Hierakonpolis and This (near Abydos), began to develop into powerful city states. At the same time there was contact, which may have been either direct or indirect, with Mesopotamia, which brought new ideas and influences into Egypt, notably writing and certain architectural forms and techniques. By the end of the period Upper Egypt had been united into one kingdom which, under Menes, defeated Lower Egypt. Thus, in about 3100 BC, Menes became the founder of the First Dynasty and the first King of Upper and Lower Egypt.

The early dynastic, or archaic, period of Egyptian history was a time of rapid development in the arts of civilization. The development of writing and written records began and the 365-day calendar was introduced. Trading expeditions reached as far south as the Second Cataract and timber was imported from Syria. Metal deposits were exploited on a large scale and magnificent stone vessels were produced. The experimental use of stone for building purposes began; the royal tombs of the first two dynasties at Sakkara were exciting and innovative, huge *mastabas* (see Glossary) of mud brick and stone. By the end of the Second Dynasty a unified Egyptian state with a strong centralized government had emerged; this, together with the great cultural advances that had been made, brought Egypt to the brink of the pyramid age.

TWO

The Pyramid Age

During the four dynasties that make up what Egyptologists term the Old Kingdom, that is, the Third Dynasty to the Sixth (*c.* 2686–2181), Egypt reached a peak of civilization that in some respects was never surpassed. By the beginning of the Third Dynasty, with internal strife at an end and no threat from abroad, the state was highly organized and efficiently administered. It was well able to make use of the country's natural resources to achieve further technological advances, and to amass yet more wealth through trade. Government was based on a court culture headed by a king who was considered to be a god. Therefore the major developments in art and architecture were brought about by the need to give expression to the cult of divine kingship, with the royal tomb regarded as the focal point of the cult. From the Third Dynasty onwards, for nearly a thousand years, royal tombs were pyramids, but those built during the Third and Fourth Dynasties are such major achievements that they justify the description of the Old Kingdom as the Pyramid Age.

The outstanding king of the Third Dynasty is Djoser (*c.* 2668–2649), whose fame lasted through the ages so that some 2,500 years after his death a decree carved on a rock on the island of Sehel[1] at Aswan purported to be issued in his name. The success of Djoser's reign was largely due to the genius of his Chief Minister, Imhotep, revered by Egyptians of later times as a sage and physician and by Greeks, who identified him with Asclepius, the god of healing, for his skill in medicine. Imhotep is thought to be the architect of Djoser's tomb, the Step Pyramid at Sakkara, the earliest-known monumental building constructed entirely of dressed stone and one of the most innovative buildings in history.

The Step Pyramid was apparently started as a *mastaba*, the traditional form of tomb at Sakkara, although with a unique square ground-plan. Its nucleus consists of a solid box-like structure made from coarse rubble set with clay mortar and faced with an outer layer of the particularly fine-grained white limestone from the quarries at Tura, some 30 km away across the Nile. A 4-m-thick casing of limestone was later added to all four sides of this square *mastaba*, finishing some 60 cms below the top edges, thus forming a small step. Along the east side eleven deep shafts were sunk into horizontal galleries which run under the superstructure. In order to cover the entrances to the shafts, which lead to the burial-places of the royal family, an enlargement of about 8½ m was made to the east side of the *mastaba*, making its shape oblong.

It seems that it was at this point that Imhotep decided upon an entirely different design. The height of the core *mastaba* was raised and three accretion walls were added around it, each outer wall being lower than the one on its inside, resulting in the first-known stepped pyramid. In the north face of this four-stepped pyramid an entrance passage was constructed. This leads to the original *mastaba*'s burial chamber, which is lined with pink Aswan granite and lies at the base of a 7-m-square shaft sunk nearly 30 m into the limestone bedrock. In the final stage in the construction of the Step Pyramid two more steps were added, making a six-stepped pyramid that is some 60 m in height, with a rectangular base measuring 120 m from west to east and 108 m from north to south.

Djoser's Step Pyramid was entirely cased in Tura limestone and must have looked like a giant wedding cake glistening in the sun. It is the focal point of a complex of buildings set, with the pyramid, within a 20-m-high rectangular perimeter wall that has a total length of over 1,625 m. The wall, which is made of limestone, was modelled on the palace façade design, possibly in imitation of the mud-brick walls of Memphis, which the ancient Egyptians called *Ineb-hedj*, 'The White Wall'. The only gateway, which is just north of the south-eastern corner, consists of a narrow passage running through the thickness of the wall. Its ceiling is made of stone blocks carved to imitate the palm logs that would have been used in earlier buildings. The passage opens into a colonnaded corridor of great originality, with columns, carved in imitation of the bundles of reeds that were normally used to support the ceilings of mud brick or wooden structures, attached to piers projecting from the side walls. At the end of the colonnade is a small hall of columns that are unique in being arranged in pairs, with the columns in each pair connected one to the other by a wall.

Most of the subsidiary buildings within the Step Pyramid's enclosure wall are without any known precedent. Adjoining the north side of the pyramid was a memorial temple, a development of the offering niche or chapel in *mastabas* and the place where funerary offerings for the dead king were made. Beside it is the *serdab* (Arabic for cellar), a sealed, box-like structure made of limestone with two small holes cut into its front wall through which the lifesized statue of Djoser housed within could, by magical means, partake of the offerings. This statue is the earliest to have been found in position. It is made of limestone, which was once painted, a technique that became the norm with limestone statues. To the east of the pyramid are two rectangular structures in which the cults of Upper and Lower Egypt were celebrated: the House of the North and the House of the South, both adorned with fluted columns engaged into their façades.

To the south of these buildings is an oblong court which contains a suite of chapels connected with the celebration of Djoser's Jubilee Festival, a ceremony which seems to have had its origins in an ancient custom observed in the predynastic period of ritually slaughtering a king to ensure the continued prosperity of the land. The purpose of the Jubilee in the dynastic period was to allow a king to escape a ritual death by renewing his powers through magic; and one of the rituals enacted during the ceremony seems to have been a race run round the walls of Memphis, represented at the Step Pyramid by the enclosure wall. Just inside the southern enclosure wall is the so-called 'South Tomb', which may have been connected with the Jubilee Festival or may have been a cenotaph representing Djoser's acknowlegement that his ancestors had been buried in Upper Egypt.

The Step Pyramid complex displays so many innovations that some have doubted that such a high degree of architectural and technical achievement could have been arrived at without a long process of development. However, there is certainly no evidence that stone had ever before been used to such an extent, and in fact many features of the Step Pyramid complex suggest that its builders lacked experience in its use, and had yet to develop independent forms suited to stone rather than to traditional materials. Accustomed to building in mud brick, they used blocks of stone that were not much larger than bricks, probably for ease of handling during construction and because they were not yet able to quarry and transport massive blocks. Supported columns such as those in the entrance corridor, or

engaged columns such as those in the Houses of the
North and South, were preferred, not for reasons of
artistic taste but because of doubts that free-standing
stone columns would be stable. The patterns chosen
for decoration were copied from materials used in
earlier buildings, with 'palm-log' stone roofs and
'reed bundle' columns.

The step pyramid begun at Meidum, some 50 km
south of Sakkara, was probably intended for Huni
(c. 2637–2613), the last king of the Third Dynasty. The
Meidum Pyramid, which marked a transitional stage
between the Third and Fourth Dynasties in the
evolution of the pyramid, originally rose to a height of
93 m, with a square base of 145 m. It was formed from
a central core of masonry around which was built a
series of accretion walls, each higher than the wall on
its outside, to form steps; but the steps were later filled
in to make a geometrically true pyramid that was
encased in Tura limestone. As in other Third Dynasty
pyramids, the blocks of stone in the accretion walls
were not bonded together but depended on sufficient
friction at the chosen angle of incline for stability. This
eventually proved insufficient to prevent the pyramid
from collapsing, although this probably did not
happen until some time during the New Kingdom,

over a thousand years later. Today the Meidum Pyramid looks like a high tower standing on a mound of rubble, and is known locally as 'the false pyramid'.

At Meidum what was to become the standard complex of buildings associated with a pyramid appears for the first time. It consists of the pyramid itself, with its entrance on the north face; a satellite pyramid, perhaps intended for a queen; and on the east side of the pyramid a memorial temple from which a causeway leads to the edge of the cultivation, to a so-called valley temple in which the king's body was prepared for burial. The valley temple was connected by canal to the Nile, along which the king's funerary cortège would have sailed. The pyramid was surrounded by a wide pavement made of mud plaster and bordered by a low wall. Since kings had forsaken the *mastaba* in favour of the pyramid, mud-brick *mastabas* were built around the pyramid for nobles. Each noble's status was reflected in the position of his *mastaba* in relation to the pyramid: the closer it was to the king's tomb, the greater the status of the owner.

Huni was succeeded by his son, Sneferu (*c.* 2613–2589). Although Sneferu was married to Hetepheres, the daughter of Huni and his chief queen,[2] he himself was the child of Meresankh, a secondary wife, and it is probably for this reason that Manetho named him as the founder of a new dynasty, the Fourth. He was a powerful and active king who became a legendary figure soon after his death, famed in literature for his geniality. In a group of stories dating to the Middle Kingdom,[3] a magician advises a bored Sneferu to go boating with the most beautiful women in his palace as his oarswomen, a suggestion the King improves upon by ordering the women to be dressed only in fishing-nets, the better to see the movements of their bodies. When the leading oarswoman loses her favourite pendant in the water and brings the rowing to a halt, the King patiently listens to her sulky refusal of his promise of a replacement and her demand that her own property be returned to her, and sends for a magician to accomplish the task. In the same story, Sneferu shows the common touch by addressing a commoner as 'my brother'; and in another[4] he calls his courtiers 'comrades'.

Sneferu had a harsher side. He was said to have led military expeditions to northern Nubia and Libya, bringing back from the former 7,000 prisoners and 200,000 head of cattle and from the latter 11,000 prisoners and 13,100 head of cattle, a surprisingly large number of captives given the population sizes of the time. Undoubtedly, many would have been sent to augment the workforce in quarries. Like his predecessors from the beginning of the Third Dynasty onwards, Sneferu was keen to exploit the copper, malachite and turquoise found in Sinai and mounted expeditions to protect Egypt's interests in the area. He also continued the contact with Byblos that had first been established in the Second Dynasty, sending trading missions to the Lebanon to obtain cedarwood. Byblos, one of the four principal towns of Phoenicia and, according to ancient Greek tradition, the oldest city in the world, was from the fourth millennium onwards an important outlet for cedarwood and other goods of interest to the Egyptians. Forty ship loads of cedar were brought to Egypt,[5] some of which was used to make doors and statues for a palace, and some to build ships. In addition to sixty small vessels, the construction of two large ships, each 100 cubits (46 m) long and presumably sea-going vessels for the Byblos trade, was recorded.

Sneferu chose Dahshur, 48 km north of Meidum, as his burial place. There he had not one but two pyramids built. The earlier, today called the Red Pyramid, was the first to be given a contemporary name, 'The Shining Pyramid'. It is the earliest structure known to have been designed from the start as a true pyramid, although its angle of incline, at 43° 40˝ shallower than the 52° or so that later became the norm, was perhaps a sign of caution on the part of its builders. To its south is 'The Southern Shining Pyramid', the only known monument of its type in Egypt. Like the Red Pyramid, it was originally about 104 m high; but its lower portion is inclined at just over 54° and its upper portion at 43° 22˝, a change in angle that was perhaps due to the need to finish the pyramid in haste, with the shallower angle requiring a smaller volume of stone. Sneferu's second pyramid is known today as the Bent Pyramid. It was cased in Tura limestone, laid not in horizontal but in sloping courses angled inwards towards the centre of the structure, a technique that gave such cohesion that most of the casing is still in place, making it the best preserved of any pyramid.

The nobles of Sneferu's court were buried in *mastabas*. Neferma'at, the architect of Huni's pyramid, was buried with his wife, Itet, at Meidum, as were Sneferu's son, Rehotep, High Priest of Re at Heliopolis (see p. 20), and his wife, Nefert. The interior walls of Neferma'at's *mastaba* were plastered and decorated with paintings, notably a large scene of Itet's two sons catching fowl in a clap net. Part of this scene, showing several geese depicted in a well-observed and naturalistic way, was undamaged when the *mastaba* was excavated, making the Meidum geese one of the earliest surviving paintings. Rehotep's *mastaba* contained the lifesized seated statues of the owner and his wife that are today regarded as masterpieces of Egyptian art. They are of painted limestone, with Rehotep's skin coloured a red-brown, indicating that he spent time in the open air, and Nefert's a pale cream, suggesting that she lived most of her life indoors.

Sneferu made a point of filling important administrative posts with members of his immediate family, a policy that was so successful that it was adopted by the kings who followed him. Neferma'at (see above), a son of either Huni or Sneferu himself, was Chief Minister, a post which, from Sneferu's time onwards, was the most important office of state, its holder second only to the king. Neferma'at was succeeded by Sneferu's son, Kanefer, who in turn was succeeded by Neferma'at's own son, Hemiunu, who became Chief Minister first of Sneferu and then of his son and successor, Khufu. The lifesized limestone statue of Hemiunu found in the *serdab* of his *mastaba* at Giza depicts him as a corpulent, middle-aged man.

Little is known about Khufu (*c.* 2589–2566), whom the Greeks called Cheops. In contrast to his father, he was viewed by later generations as an oppressive and autocratic king. In the group of stories in which Sneferu appeared as a paragon of geniality, Khufu is portrayed as one who is careless with life when he orders a magician to demonstrate on a live prisoner his ability to reattach a severed head.[6] Over 2,000 years after his death, Herodotus recounted the scurrilous claim that Khufu had been so eager to complete his pyramid that he sent his daughter to a brothel to raise the wherewithal.[7] Whatever the extent of Khufu's ruthlessness in his efforts to get his pyramid built, it is certainly the largest ever constructed, its size so impressive that it was given the name 'The Horizon'.

The original height of 'The Horizon' was 146 m (the top 9½ metres are now missing) and it covered an area of over 13 acres. It has been calculated that some 2,300,000 blocks of limestone were used in its constrution, with the weight of individual blocks ranging from 2½ to 15 tons. The pyramid, which was originally cased in Tura limestone, has three chambers, one cut into the bedrock and two within its superstructure, the result, no doubt, of changes of plan during its construction. Entrance to the uppermost chamber is gained via the so-called Grand Gallery, an ascending corridor, some 46 m long, enlarged to form a magnificent corbel vault over 8 m high. The chamber, which is lined with granite, contains the huge granite sarcophagus, now empty, in which Khufu was presumably buried.

Around the base of the pyramid are five pits, two of which, when discovered in AD 1954 and 1987, contained dismantled wooden boats. One pit has been left unopened, but the 651 component pieces of the cedarwood vessel that was in the other have been reassembled to reveal the elegant lines of a magnificent boat, 43½ m long, that is thought to have carried Khufu's body to his tomb. It is the oldest large boat so far found anywhere in the world. The precise significance of the boats that were once in the other pits is not known, but it was probably mythological, two perhaps being solar barques to allow Khufu to sail with Re (see p. 20) across the sky each day and each night, and one a vessel for making eternal pilgrimages to Abydos (see p. 32). Khufu's pyramid was extremely well levelled, planned and orientated, exciting admiration for the perfection of its workmanship. It was probably designed, as had become the norm, by the Chief Minister, in this case, Hemiunu (see above). Herodotus claimed that it was built with the labour of 100,000 slaves working in 3-monthly shifts,[8] but this figure is more likely to represent the total number of workmen employed on the pyramid during the 23 years of Khufu's reign, at the rate of about 5,000 per year. It has been estimated that about 4,000 workers were as many as could be accommodated on site at any one time, to which another 1,000 can be added to account for quarry-men and sailors. Basic labour on the pyramids was undertaken by peasants who worked for extra rations of food during the Inundation season when they could not farm their lands. None of the workers, be they the part-time peasants or the highly skilled professionals, were slaves; and many of those associated with the building of the pyramid were buried in the veritable village of *mastabas* that were constructed for them to the east and west of 'The Horizon'. These *mastabas*, which were constructed from coarse local stone faced in fine limestone, mark a departure from the traditional method of building in mud brick, and from this time onwards mud brick was used only for less important burials.

Khufu's successor was Djedefre (*c.* 2566–2558), his son, who chose Abu Roash, 8 km to the north of Giza, as the site of his pyramid. In his short reign little progress was made on it, and Djedefre is notable chiefly because he was the first king to style himself 'Son of Re'. Before the reign of Djedefre, Kings of Egypt were deemed to be gods; but in adopting the title 'Son of Re', Djedefre was allowing a diminution in his status, for he was now admitting to being merely the son of a god rather than a god in his own right. Re was the most important of the sun gods that had been worshipped in Egypt since predynastic times. His cult was established at Iunu (north-east of modern Cairo), a city which the Greeks were later to call Heliopolis (City of the Sun). From the beginning of the Old Kingdom, the cult of Re spread, enabling its priests to exert ever greater political power. The most important royal title, that of 'King of Upper and Lower Egypt', was written inside a cartouche, an elongated version of the hieroglyphic sign meaning 'encircle', to indicate that the King ruled over everything that the sun encircled during its daily cycle. The 'Son of Re' name was also written inside a cartouche. The royal association with Re was further demonstrated in pyramids, the

20

inspiration for which probably came from the mounds that were placed within the superstructures of *mastabas*, first as cores of sand overlaid with mud brick and later as solid brick constructions with four sides rising in steps. These were meant to represent the island that Egyptians believed emerged out of the primaeval ocean when the earth was created, and provided a resting place for Re.

Another of Khufu's sons, Khafre (in Greek, Chephren) succeeded Djedefre. That Egypt was prosperous during Khafre's reign (*c.* 2558–2532) is amply demonstrated in his magnificent pyramid complex, sited at Giza once again; and in an inscription in the *mastaba* of one of his sons, Nekure. The inscription, the only one of its kind from this early date, contains a copy of Nekure's will in which he left fourteen towns, at least eleven of which were named after Khafre, to his five heirs, with the proviso that the revenues of twelve of the towns be used to ensure the upkeep of Nekure's tomb and the supply of its daily offerings. Khafre's queens and children were buried, not in small pyramids and *mastabas* as Khufu's had been, but in tombs cut into the sides of the nearby quarries from which stone for his pyramid had been extracted – the earliest examples of rock-cut tombs in Egypt.

Although the ancient name of Khafre's pyramid was 'The Great Pyramid', it was a little smaller than Khufu's, its original height being 143 m. It still retains an appreciable part of its Tura limestone casing at the top and of the granite that encased its lowest course. Khafre's remarkable valley temple is an austere building devoid of decoration. The floors are paved with calcite, the walls are made of blocks of granite, or limestone faced with granite which had to be obtained from the Aswan quarries, some 1,000 km to the south, and floated down the Nile on papyrus rafts. The granite blocks are so large that it is tempting to think that the builders were trying to show what they could do with this hard stone, so much more difficult to work than the softer limestone with the tools that were available to them: work-hardened copper chisels and hard stone pounders.

Near the valley temple, an outcrop of limestone too friable to be cut into building blocks was fashioned into a lion's body with a king's head. The head may have been a portrait of Khafre; but the structure was worshipped as the god Horemakhet (Horus-on-the-Horizon) and has become a widely recognized symbol of ancient Egypt – the Great Sphinx. Lifesized statues of Khafre were placed in the valley temple, only one of which has survived. It is an austerely majestic work, sculpted in diorite-gneiss, and is unlike limestone statues in that it is polished rather than painted. It is regarded as a masterpiece of Egyptian art. There are few other statues from Khafre's reign, during which statuary was reserved for members of the royal family.

Khafre was succeeded by Menkaure (in Greek, Mycerinus) whose pyramid at Giza, which has a height of 70 m, may have been less than half the size of those belonging to Khufu and Khafre, but was intended to be cased in costly Aswan granite. However, even though Menkaure's reign of at least twenty-eight years (c. 2532–2504) should have been long enough to complete the project, only the lowest sixteen courses of the pyramid were laid in granite, with the rest cased in limestone. The memorial temple was begun in limestone with granite facing but it and the valley temple were completed in mud brick. However, several magnificent royal statues have been found in the valley temple: four slate triads of the king with the goddess, Hathor, portrayed with the face of Menkaure's queen, Khamerernebty II, and a personification of one of the Egyptian provinces. There was also a double statue of Menkaure standing with his queen by his side, her arm circling his waist, the earliest statue of this type in Egypt. The representations of the king are obviously portraits and show that he had protruberant eyes and a bulbous nose.

The small scale of Menkaure's pyramid may be an indication that the huge projects undertaken by Khufu and Khafre had depleted the royal exchequer. Nevertheless, 'The Divine Pyramid', as it was called, takes its place alongside the other two at Giza in forming one of the Seven Wonders of the ancient world. They were the last great pyramids to be built. Menkaure's successor, Shepseskaf (c. 2504–2500), returned to Sakkara to build a tomb that is not a pyramid at all but a huge rectangular structure known today as the *Mastaba el-Faraoun* (Pharaoh's Bench). His son-in-law, Ptahshepses, recorded in his *mastaba* at Sakkara that the King had accorded him a very special honour. Touching the royal person was forbidden, on pain of death, but Shepseskaf had commanded him: 'Don't kiss the ground, kiss my foot'! After Shepseskaf's death, Userkaf, a grandson of Djedefre, the short-lived successor of Khufu, inherited the throne. He married Shepseskaf's half-sister, Khentkawes, and together they founded the Fifth Dynasty.

The small scale, ranging between 43 and 70 m in height, of the pyramids built for the kings of the Fifth Dynasty was perhaps a reflection of a change of attitude and a belief that, since size had not protected the bodies of their predecessors against the depredations of tomb robbers, magic might prove more effective. Userkaf (*c.* 2498–2491) chose Sakkara as the site of his pyramid. In a departure from tradition, its memorial temple was placed on the south side of the pyramid rather than on the east, perhaps because this allowed it to be bathed in sunlight all day long. Userkaf and his successors placed great importance on the cult of the sun; and at Abu Gurob, a short distance to the north of Sakkara, Userkaf built a sun temple, a practice followed by at least four later kings.

Userkaf's successor, Sahure (*c.* 2491–2477), began a new royal cemetery at Abusir, north of Sakkara. His pyramid was not spectacular, but the walls of his memorial temple were once decorated with finely carved reliefs depicting hunting scenes and military expeditions. The most notable are those which show great ships returning from Byblos with Egyptians and Asiatics on board, early pictorial evidence of the trade with the Lebanon. Sahure was succeeded by his brother, Neferirkare (*c.* 2477–2467), who also chose Abusir as the site of his pyramid. The *mastabas* of the contemporary nobility were usually constructed at Giza and Sakkara rather than at Abusir; and the inscriptions in them add to the considerable increase in written records that occurred in Neferirkare's reign. These inscriptions sometimes throw light on court etiquette, as when Rewer, whose tomb is at Giza, records an incident in which Neferirkare hit him accidentally on the leg with his staff. The king graciously assured him that this was not a blow struck in anger and should be regarded as an honour.

In the reign of the sixth king of the Dynasty, Niuserre (*c.* 2453–2422), for whom the third pyramid at Abusir was built, it became customary to depict the ceremonial slaying of foreign chieftains as part of the decoration on the walls of a memorial temple. Niuserre made a point of recording in his funerary temples the names of a large number of his courtiers, the most notable of whom, Ti, has a very fine *mastaba* at Sakkara. The penultimate ruler of the Fifth Dynasty, Djedkare (*c.* 2414–2375), who sent expeditions to Byblos, and to Lower Nubia to obtain diorite, and for whom his Chancellor, Baurdjed, brought back a pygmy from Punt (Eritrea), chose

Sakkara once again as his burial place. His successor, Unas (*c.* 2375–2345), was also buried at Sakkara in a pyramid named 'The (Most) Beautiful of Places'.

Unas' pyramid is a landmark, for it is the earliest pyramid to have inscriptions in its interior. These inscriptions, known as the Pyramid Texts, make up the oldest body of religious literature in the world. They are found in the burial chamber and its antechamber, carved in vertical columns of hieroglyphs on a white background, each sign filled in with blue pigment so that it stands out clearly. Of a possible total of more than 700 spells in the known Pyramid Texts, Unas' pyramid has 228. The purpose of the texts was to provide a king with written descriptions of the offerings that would be made for him at his tomb and in his memorial temple; and to provide him with all the information he needed concerning the Afterlife and how to reach it.

Trade between Egypt and Byblos, Nubia and Punt, and the continuing exploitation of quarries and gold mines in Sinai and the Eastern Desert meant that the Fifth Dynasty was a time of growing prosperity. Throughout the Dynasty, however, there was a decline in royal power. For the first time, none of the known Chief Ministers was a prince; and many other high offices of state were no longer held by members of the royal family, so that full power was being taken out of their hands. A governor of a province had always been appointed by the king; but in the Fifth Dynasty, the office gradually became hereditary, leading eventually to the emergence of lines of independent rulers, who chose to be buried in fine rock-cut tombs in their own districts, evidently not feeling the necessity to be buried in *mastabas* near to the royal pyramid. Priestly power grew thanks to the endowment of mortuary priests serving great numbers of tombs; and the provision and upkeep of funerary complexes was an ever-greater charge on the royal exchequer. Each pyramid was accompanied by a sun temple, giving yet more power to the priesthood of Re.

Unas was not succeeded by a son but by the husband of his daughter, Iput. Iput's husband, Teti (*c.* 2345–2333), who apparently came from a prominent Memphite family, founded the Sixth Dynasty. He sought the good will of the nobility by arranging a marriage between his daughter, Seshseshet, and his Chief Minister, Mereruka, who was honoured with a magnificent *mastaba* built near the King's pyramid at Sakkara. Teti was succeeded by his son, Pepy I (*c.* 2332–2383), who married the daughters of a provincial nobleman from the Thinite province: confusingly, the sisters were both named Ankhnesmeryre. Pepy I also married a lady named Weretimtes, who was part of an unsuccessful conspiracy against her husband. Nevertheless, he enjoyed a long reign of nearly fifty years, and was eventually buried in a pyramid at Sakkara. It is the name of this pyramid, Men-nefer, (The Well-founded and Beautiful Pyramid) that was corrupted by the Greeks into the name Memphis, which they applied to the old capital, *Ineb-hedj* (see p. 8).

One of the most famous men of Pepy I's reign was Weni, whose career was recorded in his tomb at Abydos.[9] At one time or another Weni was Inspector of Prophets (priests) in the king's Pyramid City; a judge who conducted the inquiry against Weretimtes (see above); and a general contractor who went on many expeditions to mine stone for the king – to Tura for limestone, to Aswan for granite, to Hatnub for alabaster and, finally, to Nubia for acacia wood. The acacia wood was made into ships for the transportation of granite; and the expedition was accomplished 'in only one year' thanks to the five canals that were excavated by Weni's men to take the ships around the First Cataract. The versatile Weni also conducted a campaign against the nomads of the north-east using forces raised from all parts of Egypt, supplemented by mercenaries recruited from Nubia – the first Egyptian use of mercenaries. Although Weni claimed a great victory, it later became necessary to mount another expedition to quell an uprising among the 'sand-dwellers'. He next organized an expedition in southern Palestine during which troops were transported by ship to a place called Gazelle Nose (probably part of Mount Carmel), the first known combined land/sea operation.

Pepy I was succeeded by Merenre (c. 2283–2278), his son by Ankhnesmeryre I. Merenre reigned for only five years before being succeeded by his six-year-old half-brother, Pepy II (c. 2278–2184), the son of Ankhnesmeryre II. Pepy II's reign of ninety-four years, the longest in Egyptian history, brought the Dynasty to an end. The Sixth Dynasty had been an age of exploration, especially for the local rulers of Elephantine (Aswan) who ventured into Africa. Pepynakht, also called Hekayib, Pepy II's Overseer of Foreign Troops, recorded in his rock-cut tomb at Aswan that he had to send a force to south Nubia to quell inter-tribal fighting; and another to the Red Sea to bring back the body of an officer killed by

nomads while supervising the building of ships for
an expedition to Punt. Sabni, Pepy II's Overseer of
Upper Egypt, recorded that he had the unhappy
task of mounting a swift expedition into Nubia to
bring back the body of his father, Mekhu, who had
been killed on the Upper Nile.

The most famous explorer of the Dynasty was
Harkhuf, Overseer of Foreign Troops, who began his
career in the reign of Pepy II's grandfather and
made at least four journeys into Africa. His account
of the fourth journey, recorded at the entrance to his
tomb at Aswan, is most touching because it contains
a copy of the letter sent by Pepy II, then a boy of
about nine years old, after he had been informed
that Harkhuf was bringing back a pygmy (or dwarf)
to Egypt. The little boy's excitement breaks through
the stilted phraseology that a king was expected to
use: he tells Harkhuf to hurry to the court with the
pygmy and to set a guard on him in the boat by night
and by day to prevent him falling into the water, for
'My Majesty longs to see this pygmy more than any of
the products of Sinai or Punt.'

During the Sixth Dynasty, the expansion of
funerary provisions for the dead resulted in the
growth of the cult of Osiris, a hitherto obscure deity.

In the early part of the Old Kingdom, Re was chief judge of the dead and ruler of the Underworld; and the promise of an afterlife was at first held out only to the king and eventually to a privileged few. The myth of Osiris presented him as a beneficent king of Egypt, the shepherd of his people who was murdered by his jealous brother, Seth, and resurrected with the aid of his faithful wife, Isis. Osiris replaced Re as ruler of the Underworld. His story evoked sympathy, but he became one of the most popular deities in Egypt largely because he democratized the Underworld, holding out the promise of eternal life to everyone. His supposed burial place, Abydos, became one of the most sacred sites in Egypt.

Perhaps influenced by observing bodies preserved through natural dessication when predynastic burials were disturbed, Egyptians had come to believe that the preservation of the body was necessary for the enjoyment of an afterlife; and attempts to accomplish this by artificial means were made as early as the First Dynasty. In the predynastic period, bodies had been buried in pits dug in the porous desert sand through which the fluids of decomposition drained away before they could rot the body, while at the same time the heat of the sun conducted through the sand had dessicated the body rapidly, thus preserving it. Tombs with elaborate superstructures shielded the bodies within them from the effects of sun and sand, making them instrumental in the destruction of what they were intended to protect. In the early dynastic period, limbs were wrapped in layers of fine linen impregnated with resin in an attempt to preserve them; but the technology of true mummification, that is, the evisceration of the body to inhibit the process of decomposition, followed by rapid dessication by means of chemicals, took time to develop. The earliest mummified body is said to be that of Nefer,[10] who lived in the Fifth Dynasty and who still lies in his tomb at Sakkara.

Towards the end of the Sixth Dynasty royal power declined rapidly. In part this was due to the dead weight of maintaining the funerary monuments of previous kings and to the burden of gifts of mortuary equipment and endowments of offerings, known as *ḥtp dỉ nsw* (a gift which the king gives), which were made to nobles; and in part it was due to the longevity of Pepy II. The Dynasty, and with it the Old Kingdom, came to a end with the brief reign of Pepy II's successor, Nitocris, a female pharaoh.

THREE

The Classical Age

For nearly a century and a half power lay with provincial governors. The breakdown of central authority at the end of the Old Kingdom might have led to chaos, but Egyptian society remained essentially hierarchical and most governors managed to maintain social order in their own localities. There were no grandiose royal building projects or military expeditions, but for the first time people of quite low status owned tombs. Admittedly, the tombs were built fairly cheaply of mud brick by local craftsmen of limited ability, and most of them have long since disappeared, but the inscriptions on the many stone funerary stelae[1] that have survived paint a picture of devotion to the local ruler and gratitude for his benevolence. Nevertheless, there were sometimes serious food shortages. Autobiographical texts in the tombs of several local governors mention famine and the steps that were taken to alleviate it.[2] Ankhtify, governor of Mo'alla,[3] claimed that the starving people of Upper Egypt had been about to eat their own children until he supplied them with food.

Gradually, the rulers of Armant asserted power over the rest of Upper Egypt and founded a new dynasty, the Eleventh, which was based in *Waset*, later known to the Greeks as Thebes (modern Luxor). The Eleventh Dynasty was the first of the three dynasties that make up what Egyptologists now call the Middle Kingdom, the second great peak in Egyptian civilization. The fifth king of the Eleventh Dynasty, Mentuhotep II (2033–1982), who was viewed as a second Menes, reunited the whole of Egypt under his rule. He succeeded in bringing Nubia as far south as the Second Cataract back under Egyptian control, thus benefiting from Nubian resources and manpower. During his long, generally prosperous, reign there was renewed interest in trading and mining, and expeditions were sent to the Red Sea and Punt.

The kings of the Eleventh Dynasty used the old capital, Memphis, as an administrative centre, but they chose to be buried in Upper Egypt, on the west bank of the Nile at Thebes. The tomb of Mentuhotep II, which was built in an embayment in the cliffs occupied in Christian times by monks and known today by its Arabic name, *Deir el-Bahri*, 'the northern monastery', is one of the most unusual funerary monuments in Egyptian architecture. The tomb was integral to its memorial temple, which was made up of a *mastaba*-shaped structure surrounded by a colonnade, the whole set on a terrace approached by a ramp. The bodies of sixty soldiers, killed during an attack on a fortress, probably in Nubia, and brought back to Egypt for burial, were found in a tomb above the temple.[4]

Mentuhotep II was succeeded by his son, another Mentuhotep, who ruled for only twelve years (1982–770). During his reign the mortuary priest at the tomb of a former Chief Minister, Ipi, was a garrulous old man named Hekanakhte. Called away from home on business, Hekanakhte left his son, Merisu, in charge, but could not resist sending him letters[5] in which he fussed over his household and what they were up to. He complained that he was having to make do with 'old, dry barley' while Merisu and the rest of the family were eating 'good, new barley'; and pointed out that his household was well fed although, in a phrase reminiscent of Ankhtify (see p. 35), where he was 'they are beginning to eat men'. He ordered Merisu to make sure that his youngest son, obviously the darling of his old father's eye and a spoiled brat, was given whatever he wanted. Merisu was also ordered to get rid of a maidservant who had been causing trouble for Hekanakhte's favourite concubine. The letters were thrown on to a scrap heap near the tomb of Ipi, presumably by Merisu after he had read them, and remained there until they were discovered in AD 1921–2, when they inspired Agatha Christie to write her crime novel, *Death Comes as the End.*

Two of the outstanding officials of Mentuhotep III's reign were the Chancellor, Meketre, whose tomb at Deir el-Bahri yielded a magnificent set of funerary models representing Meketre's house and garden, his ships, his cattle and his servants; and the Chief Steward, Henenu, who led an expedition of 3,000 men through the Eastern Desert from Koptos through the Wadi Hammamat to the Red Sea, a distance of 150 km. Each man was equipped with a staff and a leather water skin – and a packtrain of donkeys accompanied the expedition, carrying sandals to replace those that were worn out on the journey. Once the Red Sea was reached, members of the expedition built a fleet of boats to take them to

Punt, where they bartered for, amongst other things, supplies of myrrh. Such an expedition took meticulous planning – trees, for example, would not have been growing on the Red Sea coast, so that timber for ship-building must either have been carried by the expedition, or stockpiled on the coast by previous expeditions. On his way back through the Wadi Hammamat, Henenu obtained graywacke from the newly reopened quarries there and set a fashion – from his time to the Thirtieth Dynasty over fifty kings sent expeditions to the quarries, and many a fine statue was made from the hard, grey-green graywacke.

The last king of the Eleventh Dynasty, Mentuhotep IV (1970–1963), sent an expedition of 10,000 men, led by his Chief Minister, Amenemhat, to the Wadi Hammamat to quarry stone for the royal sarcophagus. Rock inscriptions in the Wadi[6] record that Amenemhat was vouchsafed a miracle when a well was found full to the brim with sweet water; and that a block of stone suitable for the lid of the sarcophagus was brought to the attention of the working party by a gazelle, which gave birth upon it. The mission was very successful, completing its work in less than a month. Unfortunately for Mentuhotep

IV, he made use of his sarcophagus rather sooner than he might have wished, for less than four years after Amenemhat's return from the Wadi Hammamat, the King was dead. His Chief Minister founded a new dynasty, the Twelfth, and, deciding that Egypt could not be governed satisfactorily from Thebes, established a new capital city near the Faiyum, some 30 km south of Memphis, naming it *Amenemhat-itje-tawy* (Amenemhat-Seizer-of-the-Two-Lands), today called Lisht.

Amememhat I (1963–1934) seems to have relied upon support from district governors to attain the throne; and after becoming king he rewarded them by restoring to them their ancient title 'Great Chief'. He prevented rivalry between governors and attempts at territorial expansion by strictly delineating the boundaries of each governorate and by regulating their supplies of irrigation water from the Nile. In contrast to the kings of the Old Kingdom, he did not make the mistake of allowing the post of district governor to become hereditary but retained the right to appoint governors to office, replacing them when they died not by their own sons, who were sometimes appointed governors elsewhere, but by men from other districts. In return, local governors were required to supply on demand ships, supplies and men for royal expeditions at home and abroad.

Amenemhat freely acknowledged that his father, Senwosret, was not of royal blood, and took as one of his titles the epithet 'Wehem-Mesoot' (Repeater-of-Births), signifying that he was the inaugurator of a new era. At the beginning of his reign, Amenemhat I had two immediate problems: the legitimacy of his dynasty and the creation and training of a loyal and efficient new bureaucracy. He tackled these concerns by an intelligent use of literature, which for the first time was employed as propaganda for the furtherance of political ends. In his and succeeding reigns literary works written on papyri[7] proliferated to such an extent that the Twelfth Dynasty, which stands at the heart of the Middle Kingdom, is now regarded as the classical period of the ancient Egyptian language.

The *Prophecies of Neferty* was composed with the intent of winning support for the new king by depicting, without justification, the previous reign as a period of chaos. It purports to have been written by a contemporary of the revered Sneferu, thus cleverly linking it with a king who had a reputation for being wise and humane. Neferty foretells the advent of a saviour from Khen-Nekhen (southern Upper Egypt) called Ameny, son of a woman of Elephantine. Strangely enough, Amenemhat was born in Khen-Nekhen and his mother, Nefert, came from Elephantine. Thus Amenemhat's seizure of power was given legitimacy through the claim that his coming to the throne had been foretold. The *Book of Kemyt* (the Sum) and the *Satire of the Trades* were produced to aid recruitment to the bureaucracy. The former is a manual of scribal good practice; the latter a list of occupations, contrasted in a humorously derogatory way with the position of the scribe. Since most Egyptians were illiterate, scribes were indeed in a powerful position; according to the *Satire*, everybody had a boss, except for the scribe, who was himself the boss.

In the twenty-first year of his reign, Amenemhat I made his son, Senwosret I (1943–1898), his co-ruler, a strategem partly designed to allow the older king to delegate the more strenuous royal duties, such as military campaigns, to a younger man, but more importantly to ensure a smooth transference of power at his death. It was such a successful policy that his son and grandson were to adopt it. The young Senwosret initiated the Egyptian occupation of Nubia, establishing a fortress at Semna, near the Second Cataract, and a trading post at Kerma in northern Sudan. The wisdom of Amenemhat's policy of joint kingship was justified by the manner of his death, which seems to have been by assassination. This is described in the *Instructions of Amenemhat I*, a pseudo-autobiographical work written at the behest of Senwosret I, in which the old king describes how he was attacked at night as he lay asleep in his palace.

Another account of Amenemhat's death is found at the beginning of *The Story of Sinuhe*, one of the most accomplished pieces of narrative prose in Egyptian literature. It is the tale of Sinuhe, a courtier who was on campaign in Libya with Senwosret I when Amenemhat died. After receiving the news of his father's death, Senwosret hurries back to Egypt: but Sinuhe overhears a message being given to another of Amenemhat's sons and, fearing that he will be implicated in a plot, flees into exile. After many years of colourful adventures, Sinuhe is finally granted a royal pardon and returns to Egypt to a warm welcome from the royal family. *The Story of Sinuhe*, which was extremely popular, even hundreds of years after it was written, was an effective piece of propaganda, portraying Senwosret I as a magnanimous monarch and conveying the message that loyalty pays.

Amenemhat I and Senwosret I were both buried in pyramids built near the new capital, Lisht. The father's tomb was built on a more modest scale than that of the son, its core constructed from limestone plundered from Old Kingdom tombs at Dahshur, Giza and Sakkara. Senwosret's memorial temple was modelled on that of Pepy II, but his pyramid, which had an original height of 61 m, has a unique internal construction. Its superstructure consists of a framework of eight walls running from the centre of the pyramid, four to the corners and four to the mid-points of the sides, further divided by cross walls and filled in with rubble. Amenemhat II (1901–1866), Senwosret I's son, was buried in a pyramid at Dahshur after a long, seemingly uneventful, reign. His successor, Senwosret II (1868–1862), who inaugurated a great project of land reclamation in the Faiyum, chose to be buried at its edge, at Lahun. The most notable feature of his pyramid is that its entrance is on the south face rather than the north, its position perhaps an attempt to foil tomb robbers.

The most successful king of the Twelfth Dynasty was Senwosret III (1862–1843). His campaign in

Syria-Palestine, which he conducted in person, established the Egyptians in the area; and hymns[8] written in praise of Senwosret made much of his military exploits. He was extolled as one who 'subdues foreign lands by a wave of his hands', who 'massacres tribesmen without striking a blow and shoots an arrow without touching the bow'. Over the course of time, the three kings named Senwosret were merged in popular tradition into one, a legendary hero whose glorious deeds were so magnified that later Greek writers recounted tales of the marvellous Egyptian king, whom they called Sesostris, who conquered the world and was the greatest king ever known.

During the reigns of Senwosret III's predecessors, Egyptian control in Nubia had weakened. He began the reconquest, leading at least three expeditions in person. Eleven great mud brick forts were built in the area around the Second Cataract, blockading the river to the south. By establishing a fort at Semna, only 61 km north of Wadi Halfa, Senwosret was able to boast, 'I made my boundaries further south than those of my ancestors'; and his contempt for the Nubians is shown in the inscription on a stele set up there in the sixteenth year of his reign:

The Nubian hears only to fall at a word . . .
If one is aggressive towards him it is his back that he shows . . .
They are not people of much account.

The inscription also makes clear the real purpose of
the fort, which was to maintain an Egyptian trade
monopoly on goods such as ivory, gold and animal
skins from Africa to the south:

The southern boundary was fixed in Year 8 . . . in order to
prevent any Nubian passing it when travelling northwards by
land or by boat . . . except for any Nubian who may come to
trade in Iken (Mirgissa), or with a message – anything which
may be transacted lawfully with them but without allowing a
Nubian ship going north ever to pass by Heh (Semna).[9]

The growth of national prosperity reached its peak
in the reign of Senwosret's son, Amenemhat III
(1843–1798). With Nubia completely under Egyptian
control and many of the small countries of western
Asia acknowledging Egyptian suzerainty, and with
provincial governors posing no threat to central
authority, the King was able to turn his attention to
the economic development of Egypt. Production in
quarries and mines was increased, and expeditions to

Sinai for copper and turquoise, and to the Wadi Hammamat for graywacke, were regularly despatched. Irrigation systems were improved and the Faiyum was further developed, with an estimated 17,000 acres being added to its cultivable land by keeping the lake's feeder stream, the branch of the Nile that leaves the river near Assiut and is known today as the Bahr Yusef (Joseph's Canal), clear of silt.

The importance of the Faiyum to the rulers of the Twelfth Dynasty meant that the chief deity of the region, the crocodile god Sobek, rose to prominence. Sobek was a god of water and vegetation and in the minds of his followers associated with Osiris, the supreme god of vegetation and resurrection. Ironically he was later identified with Seth, Osiris' murderer; but in the Twelfth and Thirteenth Dynasties he was a popular god with cult centres throughout Egypt. During the reign of Amenemhat I a new state god was established. This was Amun, whose name means 'The Hidden (or Invisible) One', originally a god of the air worshipped at *Khemenu* (modern Eshmunein). A century or so before the beginning of the Middle Kingdom, the cult of Amun was introduced into *Waset* (see p. 35); and the founder of the Twelfth Dynasty, Amenemhat I, was

46

one of four kings who included the name of the god
in their own, which means 'Amun is Supreme'. The
legitimacy of the new state god was emphasized by
identifying him with the old state god, Re, as the
composite deity, Amen-Re, King of the Gods. A
temple was built for him at *Waset* and eventually *Waset*
became known as 'Newet Amon' (City of Amun),
translated in the Bible as No Amon (*Nahum* 3: 8) and
known today as Karnak.

The reigns of Senwosret III and Amenemhat III
are notable for the incomparable portrait statues of
the kings, which demonstrate a distinctive style. In
the Old Kingdom the king had been regarded as a
god, and his statues depicted him as such: he was
never portrayed as less than regal, but as an
awesome and aloof being. Twelfth Dynasty statues
were carved in a simple, traditional style, except for
the faces, which were modelled in a realistic and
eloquent way. The Dynasty had been founded by a
usurper, and its kings were conscious that they were
mortal and could, in their turn, be overthrown.
Their statues reflect these aspects of kingship, and
those of Senwosret III, in particular, portray him
with a grim face, deeply lined with fatigue and
disillusionment. The sculptors of the Dynasty were

also capable of producing exquisite raised relief, as a limestone kiosk erected at Karnak for the jubilee of Senwosret I demonstrates.

Pyramids were built at Dahshur for Senwosret III and Amenemhat III, but Amenemhat abandoned his pyramid in favour of one built at Hawara, near the Faiyum. They were constructed of mud brick cased in limestone, with concealed entrances and complex internal arrangements designed to protect them against robbery; and they were the last pyramids of any consequence to be built in Egypt. The Hawara pyramid has elaborate internal structures, but its chief claim to fame was its memorial temple which, according to Pliny,[10] had 3,000 apartments, half of which were underground, and was the original labyrinth. The subsidiary burials of royal ladies at the pyramid sites at Dahshur and Lahun, and the tombs of private individuals at Lisht, have yielded, among other things, diadems of great delicacy, necklaces and bracelets of hollow gold and semi-precious stone beads, and belts of gold beads shaped to resemble shells, all made with such fine workmanship and good taste that the Middle Kingdom can be called the classical age not only of language but also of jewellery.

Amenemhat III was the last great ruler of the
Middle Kingdom. He was succeeded by his son,
Amenemhat IV (1798–1789), who was succeeded in
his turn by his sister, Sobekneferu (1789–1786). Her
reign, like that of the Sixth-Dynasty Queen, Nitocris,
brought a great era to an end. The Thirteenth
Dynasty (1786–1633) lasted 153 years and according
to Manetho consisted of 'Sixty kings of Diospolis
(Thebes)'. The throne seems to have changed hands
on average every two-and-a-half years, never being
passed on from father to son. The office of Chief
Minister, on the other hand, became hereditary,
monopolized by the same family for generation after
generation, its holders apparently indifferent to and
unaffected by changes to the throne. It is thought
that kings were appointed and that real power lay
with the Chief Minister. In spite of this, respect for a
single central government embodied by a king
continued for some time throughout most of Egypt,
except for Xois in the western Delta, which asserted
its independence so successfully that Manetho
termed it Dynasty XIV (1786–c. 1603).

The years after the collapse of central authority at
the end of the Sixth Dynasty are remarkable for the
number of contemporary references to famine in

Upper Egypt, some apparently linked to low levels of the Nile. In contrast, Middle Kingdom graffiti at Semna, dating to about fifteen years after the death of Sobekneferu, record several years in which there were abnormally high Nile flood levels; and a stele in the temple of Amun at Karnak refers to the flooding of the temple. The disruption that such freak behaviour of the Nile brought to Egypt's capacity to be self-sufficient in food inevitably had a profound effect on the stability of the government. One outcome of this was the neglect of the eastern border, with the result that, during the last years of the Thirteenth Dynasty, in about 1650 BC, groups of people whom the Egyptians called 'Aamu' ('Asiatics'), without distinguishing them from the Asiatic tribes against whom they had long been accustomed to defend Egypt's north-eastern border, began to infiltrate into the eastern Delta.

The infiltrators were made up of several different western Asiatic peoples, including Hurrians and Indo-Aryans but, judging by their names, mainly Semites, who had for centuries been making their way southward from their original homelands east of the Caucasus mountains in Anatolia. Writing over a thousand years later, Manetho described the event as an invasion through which Egypt was seized easily without a blow being struck, after which the invaders 'burned our cities ruthlessly . . . and treated all the natives with cruel hostility'.[11] The truth was probably a lot less dramatic. Manetho called the invaders Hyksos, 'shepherds' or 'shepherd kings', but the Egyptian term for them, *hekaoo hasoot*, means simply 'rulers of foreign lands' and tells us nothing about the Hyksos except that they were not Egyptian.

The Hyksos gained control over Lower Egypt and the Delta, except for Xois where the native Fourteenth Dynasty retained its independence for some forty years. They allowed the Thirteenth Dynasty to continue to rule from Thebes, but they were able to treat it as a vassal state from which they exacted tribute. The main Hyksos group, Manetho's Fifteenth Dynasty (1648–1540), took over Memphis as its capital, while a lesser group built a capital city, *Hoot-waret* (in Greek, Avaris), in the north-eastern Delta. The eight minor chieftains in this group became Manetho's Sixteenth Dynasty (1648–1587). Little is known from contemporary written records of either group, but their regime may not have been unduly oppressive. Once in control they ruled with a firm hand and levied heavy taxes, but the native

51

dynasties in Thebes and Xois were not only tolerated but seem at times to have been on good terms with the Hyksos.

The Hyksos took over the existing machinery of administration, only gradually filling posts with Hurrians and Semites. Hyksos rulers borrowed extensively from Egyptian culture, writing their names in hieroglyphs and adopting throne names and titles. Their admiration of Egyptian art is attested by the number of statues and reliefs which they either usurped or had copied from good Middle Kingdom originals; and thanks to their respect for Egyptian learning fine copies of famous literary and scientific works were made – the Rhind Mathematical Papyrus and the Edwin Smith Surgical Papyrus are two which have survived. In return, the Hyksos may have introduced into Egypt such cultural innovations as the lyre, the vertical loom and even the *shaduf*, a frame supporting a pole with a weight at one end and a bucket at the other, which eased the lifting of water for irrigation. They also introduced the horse-drawn chariot and several new weapons, the most important of which was the composite bow, made from wood reinforced with strips of sinew and horn, thereby producing a more elastic weapon with a greater range than the simple bow the Egyptians used.

In the reign of the Fifteenth Dynasty Hyksos king, Apopi (*c.* 1560 BC), the Egyptians, led by the last two kings of what became the Seventeenth Dynasty, Seqenenre Tao II, 'the Brave', and his son, Kamose, began to reassert themselves. The only known account of the events leading up to Seqenenre's challenge to the Hyksos was written over 300 years later,[12] and perhaps should not be regarded as historically accurate. The story relates how Apopi sent a messenger to Thebes, saying: 'Come away from the hippopotamus pool. Its noise keeps me from sleeping by day and by night; its noise is in my ear.' Since Apopi was in Avaris, over 800 km from Thebes, this was obviously a pretext for war. Seqenenre was mortally wounded in battle. His mummified body, now in Cairo Museum, is badly mutilated, its head showing terrible wounds made by clubs and axes.

After Seqenenre's death, his sister-wife, Ahhotep, seems to have seized the initiative, enabling her elder son, Kamose, to continue the struggle against the Hyksos. Years later, her younger son, Ahmose, erected a stele[13] at Karnak on which she was praised very specifically:

> She is one who cares for Egypt. She has looked after its
> soldiers, she has guarded it, she has brought back its
> fugitives and collected together its deserters. She has
> pacified Upper Egypt and expelled its rebels.

Accounts of Kamose's deeds were inscribed on two
stelae at Karnak.[14] According to these inscriptions,
Apopi made an alliance with the king of Nubia and
tried to outflank Kamose by means of a pincer
movement; but his message to the Nubian was
intercepted by the Egyptians and the strategy failed.
The Hyksos were apparently not expecting a direct
attack from the Egyptians and when Kamose sailed
to Avaris, he took the city by surprise:

> I caught sight of his womenfolk upon his roof, looking out of
> their windows towards the river-bank, their bodies frozen at
> the sight of me. They looked out with their noses on their
> walls, like young mice in their holes, crying, 'It's an attack!'

When Kamose died, after a short reign of about
three years, he had control of Upper Egypt and may
have taken Memphis. It was left to his brother,
Ahmose, to complete the conquest of the Hyksos.
Egyptians were later taught to think that Hyksos rule

was a disastrous period in their history, but actually it seems to have benefited the country, not least because the invasion shook the Egyptians out of their complacent sense of inviolability against the outside world. It also provided them with an incentive for expansion; and the new Hyksos weapons played their part when the Egyptians embarked upon their great age of empire building.

FOUR

The Age of Empire

The victorious Ahmose (1550–1525) was the
founder of the Eighteenth Dynasty, the first of the
three dynasties that make up what is now called the
New Kingdom, Egypt's imperial age. Eleven years
after he came to the throne he became the first king
for over 250 years to rule over a united Egypt. His
reign was largely peaceful except for forays as far
south as Buhen (Wadi Halfa) in Nubia, undertaken
to secure Egypt's southern border. At home he
reorganized the administration: the office of local
governor was abolished in favour of giving towns
and cities their own mayors; and there was no longer
a single Chief Minister but two, one for Upper
Egypt, who ruled from Thebes, the new capital city,
and another for Lower Egypt, with a residence
in Memphis, which remained an important
administrative centre. Ahmose made a point of
rewarding officials who were loyal to him and

replacing those who were not, and seems to have treated his soldiers with great liberality.

One of those soldiers was Ahmose, son of Abana, who described his wonderful career in the biographical inscription in his rock-cut tomb at El-Kab.[1] He sailed north with the king to attack the Hyksos at Avaris and later played a valiant part in a three-year-long siege of Sharuhen,[2] in south-west Palestine. Because of his bravery, Ahmose of El-Kab was rewarded on several occasions with male and female captives and decorated with the so-called Gold of Valour. His younger relative, Ahmose Pennekheb,[3] also buried at El-Kab, seems to have had an equally illustrious career, which in his case extended over five reigns.

King Ahmose was succeeded by his son, Amenhotep I (1525–1504). In his father's reign the emphasis had been upon restoring Egypt to the Egyptians, but from Amenhotep's time there was a stated aim 'to extend the boundaries' of the country by foreign conquest. According to the accounts of both Ahmoses of El-Kab, Amenhotep mounted several campaigns in Nubia. The elder Ahmose claimed that the king captured an enemy chieftain and brought him back to Egypt in two days, which would suggest that the king did not venture very far into Nubia, probably because Nubia at that time was peaceful. A man named Turi was appointed viceroy, with the title 'King's Son of Kush', to govern the country on Amenhotep's behalf.

Amenhotep I introduced two radical changes in royal burial arrangements. For the first time the tomb was separated from its memorial temple; and, since Amun had become the state god, the pyramid form, with its associations with the sun god Re was discarded. The west bank of the Nile remained the traditional side for the burial of the dead, for it was believed that the dead went west with the setting sun; but the kings of the New Kingdom were buried at Thebes in large rock-cut tombs hewn into cliff-faces. The tombs of Ahmose and Amenhotep I are as yet undiscovered; but the fact that Amenhotep I and his mother, Ahmose-Nefertiri, were worshipped by later generations as the patron deities of the Theban necropolis would suggest that he was the first king to be buried in the valley in the limestone cliffs behind Deir el-Bahri known today as the Valley of the Kings. The site was probably selected because it is dominated by a pyramid-shaped mountain peak known to the ancient Egyptians as Meret-seger (She-

Who-Loves-Silence) and worshipped as a form of the goddess, Hathor. But the narrowness of the valley meant that there was no space in it for memorial temples, which had perforce to be constructed on the plain between the valley and the Nile. Nobles were buried in different areas of the Theban necropolis, in rock-cut tombs whose walls are decorated with lively scenes of their daily lives.

Amenhotep I had no surviving son and was succeeded by Thutmose I (1504–1492), who is thought to have been a descendant of a minor branch of the Theban royal family. On a great stele[4] erected in the second year of his reign near the island of Tombos above the Third Cataract the king claimed that his northern boundary was set on the River Euphrates; and indeed he penetrated across the Euphrates into the territory of Mitanni, a country destined to become one of Egypt's great enemies. At Nahrin, the 'River-country', a great slaughter was made;[5] and the two Ahmoses from El-Kab each captured a horse and chariot. On the way home, the king paused to hunt elephants at Niy (Apamea) in Syria. A further example of the King's prowess was observed by the doughty elder Ahmose who recorded that on campaign in Nubia, Thutmose

I shot and killed an enemy chief with his first arrow, and carried him back to Thebes hung upside down at the prow of his ship.

This great warrior pharaoh's sons by his chief wife predeceased him, and he was succeeded by Thutmose II (1492–1479), the son of a secondary wife. The new king, who was married to his half-sister, Hatshepsut, had a daughter, Neferure, by her but no son. His son was the child of a royal concubine; and when Thutmose II died it was this son who inherited the throne, the third Thutmose to do so. However, Thutmose III (1479–1425) was only a child when he came to the throne and his stepmother, Hatshepsut, became regent. To begin with, Hatshepsut kept the titles she had held as the wife of Thutmose II and allowed herself to be depicted on royal monuments standing behind her stepson. But her lineage was more royal than that of the young king; and in the second year of Thutmose III's reign, she had herself crowned as Female King.

Hatshepsut (1479–1457), who dated her reign from the death of Thutmose II, was supported by a powerful group of courtiers, notably Ahmose, the Chief Minister, Hapu-soneb, the High Priest of Amun and, above all, Senenmut. Senenmut was of undistinguished birth, but enjoyed a most remarkable career. In the reign of Thutmose II he was High Steward first to the Queen, Hatshepsut, and then to her daughter, Neferure. During Hatshepsut's reign he amassed so many offices of state that he sometimes relinquished one or two – that of High Steward to the princess Neferure, for example, he handed on to his brother, Senmen.

Senenmut's greatest achievement was Hatshepsut's memorial temple at Deir el-Bahri, which was begun in the seventh year of her reign and completed ten years later. The unique limestone temple is a series of terraces and colonnades set against a backdrop of cliffs. The flat roofs of the terraces echo the horizontal lines of the limestone beds above and the vertical lines of the columns reflect the fissures in the rock behind the temple, making it a building married perfectly to its site. Reliefs depicting important themes from Hatshepsut's life decorate walls in the colonnades: her birth, her coronation, a great expedition to Punt and the transportation of two obelisks for the Temple of Amun in Thebes. It was Senenmut who was in charge of transporting these granite needles, each nearly 30 m high, which were carried downstream from Elephantine (Aswan) to Thebes strapped end to end on a sledge placed on a huge barge made of sycamore wood. The barge was towed by 27 ships with 864 oarsmen. In the fifteenth year of her reign, Hatshepsut commissioned another pair of obelisks of similar size, this time appointing her steward, Amenhotep, as leader of the expedition which lasted for just seven months. One of these obelisks still stands in the Temple of Amun at Karnak.

In the birth scenes at Deir el-Bahri, Hatshepsut justified her seizure of the throne by claiming that although she was the daughter of her earthly father Thutmose I, she was also the divine child of the god, Amun, begotten by him on Thutmose's queen and chosen by him as heir to the throne of Egypt. For good measure, Hatshepsut claimed in an inscription elsewhere in the temple that Thutmose I had assembled his courtiers and announced that his daughter was to be king. The coronation scenes were equally fictitious, for they show Hatshepsut being crowned during the lifetime of her father. The expedition to Punt,[6] however, was not an imaginary one. Five ships set out from a port on the Red Sea (possibly Quseir) to journey southwards to Suakin, where the expedition disembarked to travel inland.

The voyage took about twenty days, covering on average about 50 km a day, with the ships hugging the coast rather than risk the dangerous deep water of the Red Sea. In Punt the Egyptians traded a few weapons and some trinkets for sacks of aromatic gum, gold, ebony, ivory, leopard skins, live apes and, above all, myrrh trees. These were taken back to Egypt, their roots packed in baskets, and replanted in the courtyard of the temple at Deir el-Bahri.

At Hatshepsut's death in 1457 no Egyptian armies had been in western Asia for over twenty years. Babylon and the petty kingdoms of Syria-Palestine had become weak; but the Mitannians (see p. 59) were attempting to move south towards Egypt. Thanks to Hatshepsut Egypt was prosperous and well organized, and Thutmose III was ready to meet the challenge posed by Mitanni. Over the next thirty-two years he fought the seventeen campaigns[7] which established an Egyptian empire in western Asia and made him the epitome of the warrior pharaohs who were such a distinguishing feature of the New Kingdom.

By the reign of Thutmose III the Egyptian army had developed on a national basis into a well-organized service manned by professionals and supported by a plethora of scribes. Soldiers were recruited by conscription and the training of new recruits, which seems to have consisted of drill practice combined with physical punishment, was carried out in special camps. The army consisted of infantry and an élite corps of chariotry, with three or four divisions each divided into twenty companies, with five platoons of fifty infantrymen. Each division of 5,000 men was under the control of a general, who was usually a royal prince. The Commander-in-Chief was, of course, the king himself. Although the complex hierarchy of officers was normally recruited from men of standing, men of ability could work their way up through the ranks.

Mitanni supported an alliance of Egypt's enemies in western Asia that was led by Kadesh, a city on the River Orontes in Syria. Thus Thutmose III had to deal with Kadesh before challenging the Mitannians. In his first campaign he launched an attack across Sinai into Palestine, up to the ridge of Mount Carmel and thence to Gaza. The key city of Megiddo lay 150 km north of Gaza, which Thutmose realized he must capture before proceeding any further. By taking a route through a defile in the hills against the advice of his war council, who had exclaimed:

'How can we go upon this road which threatens to be narrow? . . . Will not horse come behind horse and man behind man likewise? Shall our advance-guard be fighting while our rear-guard is still standing in Aruna waiting to fight?', he took the army of Megiddo by surprise. To Thutmose's annoyance the routed army scrambled back into the city while the Egyptians stopped to plunder the battlefield, forcing him to lay siege to Megiddo for seven months. Eventually the city fell. In the Battle of Megiddo Thutmose displayed one of the pre-requisites of a successful general – he was lucky, but it could have been otherwise. In the Bible,[8] Megiddo is named Armageddon, site of the last great battle.

The next six campaigns were to consolidate Egypt's hold on conquered territories and to make preparations for the great push against Kadesh. Kadesh was taken in 1509 BC, and in the thirty-third year of his reign Thutmose fought the eighth and greatest of his campaigns. He sailed to Byblos and marched through the Lebanese mountains to the Orontes valley. Having defeated the King of Mitanni at Aleppo, Thutmose chased the Mitannian army across the Euphrates and sailed up and down the river on boats that had been dragged from Byblos via Aleppo, a journey of over 400 km. He did not, however, pursue the Mitannians into their heartland, wisely contenting himself with drawing a line at the Euphrates. During the journey back to Egypt Thutmose III, like Thutmose I before him (see p. 59), found time for some big-game hunting at Niy, where he encountered a herd of 120 elephants. In the ensuing slaughter the largest tusker turned on the King, who was saved by the prompt action of Amenemhab,[9] one of his officers, who leaped forward and cut off its trunk. Thutmose's next eight campaigns were mainly tours of inspection, but in the forty-second year of his reign Kadesh revolted and he was forced to mount one last campaign, his seventeenth. There was a stubborn defence of the city. When the prince of Kadesh let loose a mare in front of the Egyptian army with the intention of unsettling the stallions in his enemy's chariotry, the resourceful Amenemhab sprang into action, chasing her and slitting open her belly, after which he cut off her tail and presented it to Thutmose. Inevitably, it was Amenemhab who was the first to breach Kadesh's defences.

Thutmose III, a man of diverse abilities and talents, was modest, his inscriptions being much less bombastic than those of less accomplished rulers. An excellent general and a competent administrator, he seems also to have been a fine charioteer, archer and athlete. He encouraged and promoted art and architecture and his buildings, especially the Festival Hall built for him at Karnak, and his tomb, with its beautiful cartouche-shaped burial chamber, were models of restraint and good taste. Unusually for his time, he took an interest in natural history and ordered a vestibule at Karnak to be decorated with reliefs depicting the animals and 'plants that his Majesty encountered in the land of Syria-Palestine.'

During Thutmose's reign Memphis was reinstated as *de facto* capital of Egypt, mainly because it was better than Thebes as a starting point for expeditions to western Asia. Egypt's effective frontier was pushed far beyond its natural borders, making the country secure and opening up other regions to trade and commerce. The wealth this brought developed in the Egyptians a taste for luxury and broadened their minds so that they ceased to be inward looking and became willing to accept new ideas. The foreign goods which poured into Egypt introduced Egyptian craftsmen to new artistic forms.

Foreigners arrived in Egypt in large numbers, bringing with them deities such as Baal, Anat and Astarte, who were assimilated into the Egyptian pantheon, different customs and styles of dress, and foreign words that were incorporated into the Egyptian language. The successful army created a powerful military class; and the foreign tribute which percolated through to large numbers of temples created an even more powerful priesthood. High priests had control not only of great wealth but also of great estates. The priesthood of Amun in particular received an enormous amount of the wealth obtained from the Empire thanks to the patronage of Thutmose III who, as a child, had been their protégé.

Thutmose III's death was the signal for revolt in the Asiatic empire. It was put down by his son and successor, Amenhotep II (1427–1393), who captured Tahsi, near Kadesh. He made an example of seven enemy princes, whom he claimed to have slain with his own mace, by hanging them upside down at the prow of his ship and afterwards displaying six of them in front of the walls of Thebes, and one on the wall at Napata, in Nubia, 'in order to display His Majesty's triumph'.[10] It was never necessary for

Amenhotep II to emulate the military exploits of his father, but he did make much of his military training. Near the Great Sphinx at Giza a stele[11] records his prowess: by the time he was eighteen years old he had mastered the arts of war and had such a profound understanding of horses that his father put him in charge of the royal stables, where he handled horses so skilfully that they were able to run long distances without sweating! He was so strong that on one occasion, when he was being rowed by 200 men who became tired, he seized an oar himself and, so he claimed, rowed six times as far as they had done. He tested 300 strong bows and shortly afterwards, mounted on his chariot, shot at speed at four copper targets, his arrows hitting them so hard that they pierced each target through to the back.

It seems that Amenhotep II's successor, Thutmose IV (1392–1383), was not the original crown prince; but, on a stele erected between the paws of the Sphinx, Thutmose IV related how, in a dream, the Sphinx promised him the throne if he would clear away the sand that was encroaching upon it. This he did and duly became king. During his reign the growing power of the Hittites of Anatolia was seen as a threat not only to Egypt but also to its old enemy, Mitanni. As a result Thutmose IV sought an alliance with Artatama I, King of Mitanni, and asked for his daughter's hand in marriage. For nearly forty years there was peace in the Asiatic empire. The warrior pharaohs of the early Eighteenth Dynasty had established Egypt as the dominant power in the Near East; diplomacy had taken the place of warfare.

When the next King of Egypt, Amenhotep III (1383–1345), came to the throne, Egypt was at the height of its power and prosperity, the richest country on earth. Amenhotep had ample opportunity to indulge his taste for opulence and display and initiated a great programme of temple building, not only in Egypt but also in Nubia where, in the temple at Soleb, he was actively deified in his own lifetime. At Thebes, his memorial temple was said to be made from 'fine white limestone, wrought with gold throughout'. It was embellished with granite statues of the king, eighteen of which still survive, and its entrance was flanked by two sandstone statues of Amenhotep, each some 18 m high, known today as the 'Colossi of Memnon'.

Amenhotep III made several diplomatic marriages, but at the beginning of his reign he married Tiy, the daughter of Yuya, who held important priestly office in the city of Akhmim. Tiy was a commoner, but despite this she exerted considerable influence, both personal and political, a fact recognized by at least one foreign king, Tushratta of Mitanni, in the letters[12] he wrote to her after Amenhotep III's death. Throughout their long marriage, Tiy was fêted by her husband, who had a temple built for her at Sedeinga, in Nubia, where she was worshipped in her own lifetime. However, Amenhotep's high regard for Tiy did not prevent him marrying one of their daughters, Sitamun, by whom he had children.

During Amenhotep III's reign the situation in western Asia began to change. Egypt's ally, Mitanni, was engaged in a desperate struggle against the Hittites and the Assyrians, who had become more powerful and were trying to suborn the petty princelings of Syria-Palestine. Even Thutmose III would have had difficulty with these new states, which were more proficient at war than Egypt's old enemies had been; but Amenhotep III was disinclined to mount military operations. Events abroad only exacerbated the situation in Egypt which was one in which the priesthood of Amun, made ever more powerful during the reigns of Thutmose III and his son and grandson, was beginning to present a major threat to the throne. Amenhotep III took steps to reduce its power by favouring the sun god Re, and by appointing men from Memphite families who had no loyalty to Amun to posts in Thebes. His most determined move against Amun, however, was to set up a minor sun god, Aten, as the god of empire.

Some eight years before his death, an ailing Amenhotep III made his son, Amenhotep IV, his co-ruler. Amenhotep IV (1353–1337) was no more a warrior pharaoh than his father had been. He chose to ignore what was happening in the Empire and to concentrate on countering the power of Amun by promoting the cult of Aten. A new concept of divine kingship was formed in which king and god were indivisible. Statues of the king depict him as an hermaphrodite, a god who was both father and mother; and emphasis was placed on the kingship of Aten, whose name was written inside a cartouche as though he were an earthly king. Amenhotep IV has often been presented as the first monotheist, a visionary inspired by his new god, Aten; but his religious revolution was, rather, an attempt to use religion for political purposes by a king who was unable or unwilling to use secular means.

In the fifth year of his reign, the king changed his name from Amenhotep (Pleasing-to-Amun) to Akhenaten (Glorious-Spirit-of-the-Aten); and a year later ordered a new city to be built some 330 km north of Thebes. It was called Akhetaten (Horizon-of-the-Aten), better known today as Amarna. There, Akhenaten lived with his wife, Nefertiti, famed for her beauty, and their six daughters, surrounded by sycophantic courtiers who were rewarded with tombs cut into the cliffs that border the desert edge to the east of the city. In these tombs, which are largely decorated with scenes of the royal family out and about among its loyal and adoring retainers, the distinctive Amarna art style is seen to great effect.

By the ninth year of his reign Akhenaten had proscribed the old gods of Egypt and closed down their temples. Such religious persecution was new to the Egyptians, who had always worshipped many deities and been ready to add new gods to the pantheon. Officially, although not in fact in practice, the Egyptians were left with Atenism, a very exclusive religion confined to the royal family, with the king as the only mediator between mankind and

Aten. The closure of temples was an even more serious matter. Although Egyptian temples were not centres of congregational worship, and most Egyptians were not permitted to enter them, they played an important part in the economic and social life of the community. Temples owned great estates and rented land to peasant farmers; their precincts contained schools which produced scribes, doctors and artists. The services of temple scribes could be obtained whenever the local population, most of whom were illiterate, had need of them to draw up wills, write legal documents or compose letters; and physician-priests who were based in temple precincts offered a rudimentary health service. Akhenaten's closure of these institutions must have inflicted great hardship on the Egyptians.

In the twelfth year of his reign Akhenaten held a great reception in Akhetaten in which he received tribute from the Empire. It was a deception: for years, desperate rulers of the city states in western Asia had been sending requests for help against the Hittites and their allies to Akhenaten, who either ignored them or perhaps was not permitted by over-zealous officials to see them. Egypt's most loyal ally, Ribaddi of Byblos, sent over fifty letters[13] to

Akhenaten asking for help against Abdiashirta of Amor, and later against Abdiashirta's son, Aziru. Ribaddi warned that 'Abdiashirta is a cur and he is seeking to capture all the cities of the king' and claimed that Akhenaten's inaction was allowing Byblos to 'go out of his hand'. Ribaddi entreated Akhenaten in vain to send him 20 pairs of horses and 300 men, for 'thus will we be able to hold the city'; but, for the lack of such a pitifully small amount of aid, Byblos was lost.

About a year before he died Akhenaten made his brother Smenkare (1338–1336) joint ruler; but within two years both Akhanaten and Smenkare were dead; and Smenkare's ten-year-old brother, Tutankhaten, came to the throne, changing his name to Tutankhamun (1336–1327). Presumably on the advice of his ministers, Tutankhamun moved back to Thebes and reinstated the cult of Amun. Apart from allowing Amun's priesthood to be restored to power, he achieved little and was a king who 'spent his life making images of the gods'. As far as the modern world is concerned, however, Tutankhamun is the most famous king ever to rule Egypt because, in AD 1922, his tomb was found almost intact. His reign lasted for only nine years

75

and he was succeeded by Tiy's brother, the elderly Ay (1327–1323). At Ay's death, the chief general of the army, Horemheb, inherited the throne, perhaps because the army had decided that it was time to intervene before the whole Asiatic Empire was lost.

Horemheb (1323–1295), even while still a general, had been instrumental in attempts to regain the Empire; and a magnificent tomb built for him at Sakkara[14] during the reign of Tutankhamun was a fitting acknowledgement of his achievements as a military commander in campaigns in Syria, Nubia and possibly Libya. He held no truck with the four previous kings and dated his reign from the death of Amenhotep III. Horemheb was an efficient and successful king but, having no son, he was forced to appoint an elderly fellow general as his successor. Thus Ramesses I (1295–1294) became the founder of the Nineteenth Dynasty and after a reign of sixteen months was succeeded by his son, Sety.

Sety I (1294–1279) was one of Egypt's greatest kings. He reconquered much of the empire won by Thutmose III, even recapturing Kadesh, held by the Hittites. This encounter between Egypt and the Hittites is the first known battle between two countries that had been enemies for years but had never before come face to face in war. Sety 'made a great slaughter among the wretched Hittites . . . slaying their chiefs, overthrown in their own gore'; and then made a peace treaty with them. His campaigns were recorded on the north and east exterior walls of the Hypostyle Hall (see below) at Karnak.[15] Unlike earlier records, such as the Annals of Thutmose III, Sety's campaigns are set down in a mixture of hieroglyphic inscriptions and reliefs depicting the king's activities, a way of depicting historical events that initiated a new form of Egyptian art.

Artistic standards reached a new height in Sety's reign. The walls of his tomb, which is the finest in the Valley of the Kings, are decorated with reliefs of a quality that is matched only by those in a temple that was built for him at Abydos. The Abydos temple, the greatest architectural achievement of Sety's reign, is unusual in two ways: it is L-shaped; and it was dedicated to seven deities: Osiris, Isis and Horus, Amun, Ptah and Re-Horakhty, and to Sety I himself. It is perhaps the most beautiful of all Egyptian temples; but the Hypostyle Hall, Sety's contribution to the Temple of Amun, makes Karnak the most spectacular. At Karnak Sety ordered a magnificent columned hall of 122 sandstone columns, each 15 m high, to be arranged in rows on either side of the huge colonnade of 12 columns that had been built for Amenhotep III. The columns in the central aisle, each 22 m high with a circumference of nearly 10 m, have capitals shaped like open papyrus umbels, while the surrounding columns have capitals representing lotus buds; both types are typical of the Egyptian custom of basing architectural patterns in stone on ancient vegetable prototypes. Since the Egyptians did not use a keystone in their stone buildings, which therefore never feature stone arches, each column in the Hypostyle Hall was set at a critical distance from its neighbour, close enough to allow the stone slabs with which the hall was originally roofed to be laid on top of the columns without cracking under their own weight. The hall is surrounded by a wall and a planned difference in height between the central columns and those on either side allowed clerestory window gratings to be inserted along the length of the central nave.

Sety I was succeeded by his son, Ramesses II (1279–1213), thought by some to be the greatest Egyptian king although he himself sought to emulate Thutmose III, a rival candidate for the epithet. For Thutmose III the capture of Megiddo was the key to his success against his enemies the Mitannians; for Ramesses, the Hittites were the enemies, and Kadesh was his equivalent of Megiddo. Kadesh had been lost to the Hittites and in the fifth year of his reign, Ramesses set about reconquering it. He led the Egyptian army, whose four divisions at this period were named after the gods Pre, Ptah, Sutekh and Amun, along the coast of Palestine until they reached the land of Amor. It then turned inland, marched along the Litani valley, and camped about a day's march from Kadesh. The next day Ramesses, at the head of the Division of Amun, pushed on until he was about 13 km south of Kadesh, his way blocked by the River Orontes, which had to be crossed by the Shabtuna ford. Before the crossing was made two captured bedouin were brought into camp and questioned. They reported that the Hittite army was not at Kadesh but 200 km to the north at Halab (Aleppo). Ramesses believed them and rashly dashed off with only the Division of Amun, making camp just to the north-west of Kadesh. No sooner had he done so than another two bedouin were brought in and revealed the alarming truth that the Hittites were not at Halab at all, but hidden to the north of Kadesh.

Ramesses immediately sent messengers to the Division of Re with orders for it to advance quickly, but the Hittites attacked from the southern side of Kadesh, catching the division unprepared and cutting through it. The survivors dashed into Ramesses's camp, where he was sitting with his officers upbraiding them for what had happened, and threw it into panic. When the Hittites arrived in pursuit Ramesses was surrounded by enemies with only his bodyguard to protect him. He charged out of camp through the Hittite lines and, fortunately for him, the Hittites, like Thutmose III's army at Megiddo, stopped to plunder. At this point, a body of troops from Amor arrived. They engaged the Hittites in the camp while Ramesses rallied the remains of his two divisions for an attack. The Egyptians charged the Hittites six times and the Hittite commander launched a further thousand chariots, but to no avail: they were driven into the Orontes. The battle lasted over three hours and in that time the Division of Ptah had made up ground and eventually came charging to the rescue. The Division of Sutekh never arrived at all – what

Ramesses said to its commanding officer is not recorded. Once darkness fell the fighting was over. The Hittite king, Muwatallish, had kept between 8,000 and 9,000 foot soldiers in reserve, presumably because he could not believe that the foolhardy action of Ramesses in not keeping the Egyptian army divisions together was not part of an elaborate trap.

The next day a truce was called. Strategically, the result of the Battle of Kadesh was a defeat for the Egyptians: they failed to capture the city and were forced to return to Egypt with nothing to show for their efforts. Ramesses, who was lucky not to have been killed, declared at the time that the battle was a draw. But for the sixty-one years that remained of his reign, accounts of the Battle of Kadesh and of how, almost single-handed, he had won it, were a constant refrain, especially on his public monuments. Sixteen years after the battle, a peace treaty was drawn up between the Hittites and Egypt in which both sides agreed to renounce all territorial ambitions in favour of peace reinforced by a mutual defence pact. The treaty also made the first known provision for the exchange of political refugees. For the rest of Ramesses's reign relations between the two countries were good: the kings, and their queens, wrote to each other; and the Hittite king, Hattusil, even contemplated a state visit to Egypt. When Ramesses was in his mid-sixties one of Hattusil's daughters was sent to Egypt to be his bride; and a few years later he married a second Hittite princess.

Ramesses II was a great builder: monuments constructed, completed or enlarged during his reign include his own and his father's temple at Abydos, his father's memorial temple at El-Qurna (Thebes), the Temple of Ptah at Memphis, the Temples of Amun at Luxor and Karnak, and several temples in Nubia including two imposing rock-cut temples at Abu Simbel, one for himself, the other for his wife, Nefertiri, for whom was constructed what is perhaps the most beautifully decorated tomb in Egypt. Ramesses's own tomb, in the Valley of the Kings, is large and his memorial temple, the Ramesseum, a combination of palace and temple, was impressive. In the eastern Delta Ramesses built a new city, *Pi-Ramessu* or the City of Ramesses, which, according to contemporary descriptions, was beautiful beyond compare. Many statues of Ramesses were erected throughout Egypt, the largest being the granite colossus, originally weighing 1,000 tons, that now lies in pieces in the courtyard of the Ramesseum. His throne name, *wsr-maat-Re*, was corrupted by the Greeks into Ozymandias, of whom the poet Shelley pertinently wrote: 'Look on my works, ye mighty, and despair!'[16]

A comparison between Ramesses's mummy, which has survived, and his statues shows that he was handsome and physically imposing. He was over ninety years old when he died, the length of his reign outmatched only by that of Pepy II. During that time he fathered numerous children – at least forty-nine of his sons and thirty-eight of his daughters are known by name, while many others remain anonymous. He had several Great Wives or Queens-in-Chief, at least two of whom were his daughters, but the most illustrious was Nefertiri (see above). It was not she, however, but Isinofret who was the mother of Merenptah (1213–1203), his thirteenth son, who eventually succeeded him.

In the fifth year of Merenptah's reign, Libyans formed a coalition with tribes from the coasts and islands of Asia Minor and the Aegean – the so-called Sea Peoples. Driven by the need to find food and a place to settle, they mounted an invasion of Egypt which, after a six-hour battle, was repulsed. The seventeen years after Merenptah's death were times of weakness and disorganization, and in 1186 BC, the Nineteenth Dynasty collapsed.

Ramesses III (1184–1153), the second king in the Twentieth Dynasty who, it is thought, survived a conspiracy against his life,[17] had a magnificent tomb built in the Valley of the Kings and an even more magnificent memorial temple. The latter, which was called 'United with Eternity' but is now known as Medinet Habu, had two splendid palaces on its south side and became the administrative centre for the whole Theban necropolis. On the walls of the temple the battles of Ramesses III, the last of the warrior pharaohs, were recorded. In the fifth year of his reign, the Sea Peoples returned to Egypt and, after six years of struggle, were finally defeated. Ramesses, however, may have won the battle but in doing so he lost the war, for some of the tribes took over Egypt's empire in western Asia and with it access to major sources of iron, the metal that was to revolutionize the first millennium BC. Their expertise in iron working enabled the civilized world to move into the Iron Age while Egypt, for a crucial period, remained stranded in the Bronze Age.

FIVE

The Last Pharaohs

The last eight kings, all called Ramesses, of the Twentieth Dynasty ruled over a country that had been exhausted in the struggle against the Sea Peoples and was suffering increasing economic and social distress. Loss of empire meant a huge fall in revenue, there was a smallpox epidemic in the reign of Ramesses V (1147–1143) and under Ramesses VIII (1129–1126) grain was highly priced and often in short supply, at times leading to famine. During the reign of Ramesses IX (1126–1108) there was an increase in the robbery of royal tombs. Strenuous efforts were made to protect them and the royal mummies were successfully saved from destruction. Tomb robbers were caught and brought to trial, records of which have been preserved on several papyri.[1]

Many of the tomb robbers were men connected with a village close to the Valley of the Kings, known today as Deir el-Medina. The village had been constructed in the Eighteenth Dynasty specifically to house the workmen of the royal necropolis. Documents written for the families who lived in Deir el-Medina[2] provide a great deal of information about the preparation of royal tombs and the lives of the men who worked on them. These documents prove that far from being slaves the workmen were skilled and valued craftsmen who not only enjoyed a privileged lifestyle by ancient Egyptian standards but were prepared to express discontent when they felt it was necessary. In the Twentieth Dynasty the workmen had on occasion to complain about the late or non-delivery of their supplies; and when their complaints were ignored, they went on strike.[3]

Towards the end of the Twentieth Dynasty the priesthood of Amun once more proved to be a threat to the throne. At Karnak a relief showing Ramesses IX rewarding the High Priest, Amenhotep, is instructive: both figures are carved on the same scale and therefore, according to the conventions of Egyptian art, were of equal importance. In the reign of Ramesses XI (1099–1070/69), the High Priest, Herihor, was also Chief Minister. He decreed that the office should be held by his descendants in perpetuity, with the result that the Twenty-first Dynasty was divided into two. High Priests ruled Upper Egypt from Thebes and a collateral branch of the Herihor family, founded by Smendes (1070/69–1043), ruled from Tanis in the eastern Delta, at first over Lower Egypt only but later over the whole land.

Smendes's son, Psusennes I (1039–991), used Ramesses II's city, *Pi-Ramessu*, as a quarry for the construction of temples and palaces in Tanis. His tomb, like several others, was sunk into the ground as a stone-lined chamber and was found almost intact in AD 1940.[4] The kings were buried in magnificent granite or quartzite sarcophagi, sometimes usurped from earlier rulers, and silver mummy cases. Funerary equipment, especially vessels of gold and silver and jewellery, was simple and elegant.

The Twenty-first Dynasty was overthrown by the descendants of Libyan mercenaries who had settled in the region of Herakleopolis. The outstanding figure of the Twenty-second Dynasty was its first king, Sheshonq (945–924), who established his capital at Bubastis in a strategically important position controlling the routes through the eastern Delta between Memphis and Sinai. He conducted a successful campaign in Palestine, and hence is mentioned in the Bible under the name Shishak; but the later years of the Dynasty were times of civil war, when rival dynasties were set up in Leontopolis (Dynasty XXIII) and Sais (Dynasty XIV). Thus it was a relatively easy matter for the Kushite (Sudanese) king, Piyi, to intervene and by 747 BC he had control of Egypt from Thebes southwards.

Initially, Piyi (747–716) seems to have thought in terms of a protectorate rather than of direct rule, but the political ambitions of local princes forced him to occupy the whole of Egypt. After his death, his brother Shabaka (716–702) became king, resident in Egypt and true founder of the Twenty-fifth, Kushite, Dynasty. The greatest need during the Dynasty was to establish a buffer on Egypt's eastern border against the Assyrians, but the Kushites tended towards parocialism, and were too often absent in Kush when the situation in Egypt needed their attention. Taharqa (690–664) was the most active militarily, but he was outmanoeuvred by the Assyrians and in 669 BC was defeated by Asshurbanipal. His successor, Tantamani (664–656), regained possession of Egypt, but then returned to Kush and was there when the Assyrians sacked Thebes in 663 BC.

The Assyrians installed a Saite prince as governor of Egypt, but his son, Psammeticus I (663–610), gradually made Egypt independent of Assyria. He founded the Twenty-sixth Dynasty under which Egypt enjoyed over a century of relative power and prosperity. The Saite Period was a cultural renaissance in which there was a conscious spirit of archaism, a return to the great days of Egyptian art and architecture and a revival of things such as animal worship that were peculiarly Egyptian. The economic and military power of the Dynasty was brought about largely through its encouragement of Greek traders and the building up of the navy for mercantile and military purposes. The army was underpinned by the judicious use of Greek mercenaries.

Egypt was finally brought into contact with the might of the Persian Empire. In 525 BC Cambyses defeated the last king of the Twenty-sixth Dynasty, Psammeticus III (526–525), and the Twenty-seventh Dynasty was actually one of direct Persian rule. Under Darius I (521–486) the rule was not unduly oppressive, but the harshness of later kings provoked the Egyptians to rebellions that were unsuccessful until the revolt of the Saite prince,

Amyrtaios. He freed Egypt from the Persians and from 404 to 399 was the sole ruler of the Twenty-eighth Dynasty. Then, for sixty-one years, Egypt maintained a precarious independence, first under the kings of the Twenty-ninth Dynasty, who ruled from Memphis, and then under the Thirtieth Dynasty, based in Sebennytos. In 360 BC Nectanebo II (360–343) became the last native king to rule Egypt until, in 343 BC, the Persians conquered the country once more. The second period of Persian domination came to an end in 332 BC with the victory of Alexander the Great at the Battle of Issus, when Egypt became part of his Macedonian Empire.

Postscript

The Egyptians produced one of the world's greatest civilizations, one that lasted for over 3,000 years, the product of a society that has been described, aptly, as pyramid shaped. At the apex of the pyramid was the King, just below him was a narrow segment of nobles and below them a slightly wider stratum of scribes and craftsmen. The largest part of the pyramid was occupied by the mass of the people who were simple, illiterate peasants who worked in the fields. The King was regarded as a god who nevertheless was subject to the rule of law. It was said that when the world was created the sun god, Re, came down to earth to reign as King of Egypt, bringing with him his daughter, Maat, the personification of Truth, Order and Justice. Thus these three concepts came to earth at the same time as the concept of kingship; and in Egyptian eyes they were inextricably linked.

As a people the Egyptians were peaceable and gregarious, with a love of life and a sense of humour. They had to work hard to reap the benefits of a land that was usually wonderfully fertile but could, during periods of low Nile Inundations, suffer drought. Most had a short life span by modern standards – an average of about thirty years – and their health was adversely affected by their living conditions, with intestinal worms and parasites and eye and lung diseases constant scourges. They were tolerant, religiously and domestically; and Egyptian women enjoyed a degree of freedom and autonomy that has seldom been equalled. So, perhaps it is fitting that this brief history of Ancient Egypt should end with a love poem[5] or two:

When I think of your love
My heart stands still within me
If I see sweet cakes
They seem like salt
And pomegranate-wine, so sweet in the mouth
Is like bird's gall to me
Your kiss alone
Is what brings my heart to life

My heart sings
Whenever we walk together
Listening to your voice is like pomegranate-wine
I come alive when I hear it
Every glance you cast my way
Means more to me than food or drink.

Glossary

cartouche Ornamental oblong shape, representing a loop of rope knotted at the base, used in hieroglyphic inscriptions to identify the last two names in the royal titulary.

Dynasty The divisions into which Egyptian history was divided by the scholar priest Manetho in the third century BC: roughly familes of kings akin to Tudors or Stuarts.

mastaba **(Arabic)** Rectangular mud brick bench with battened sides sometimes found outside village houses in Egypt. Term applied to describe royal tombs of the first two dynasties and private tombs of the Old Kingdom, which are similar in shape.

memorial temple Temple dedicated to the worship of a dead king.

mortuary temple see memorial temple

necropolis Cemetery literally 'city of the dead' from Greek *nekros* (corpse) *polis* (city).

obelisk Shaft of stone (usually granite) with pyramid-shaped top; from Greek *obeliskoi* (little spits).

predynastic Period of Egyptian history that predates writing and the unification of the country into one state. The prehistoric period before 3100 BC.

pyramid Royal tomb in use in Egypt from Dynasty III to Dynasty XVII.

sarcophagus Stone coffin, from Greek *sarco* (flesh) *phag* (eat, swallow); literally 'flesh-eater' because of the custom during certain periods of Greek history to cover bodies within stone coffins with quicklime.

stele (or stela), plural: stelae Slab of stone, usually rectangular in shape with curved top, decorated with relief and inscription.

Notes

INTRODUCTION

1. Not to be confused with the European sycamore (*Acer pseudoplatanus*), a maple tree; or with the North American sycamore (of the genus *Platanus*), a plane tree.

CHAPTER TWO

1. Lichtheim, III, p. 94.
2. For an account of royal marriage in ancient Egypt see Watterson, 1991, p. 148ff.
3. *The Westcar Papyrus*; see Lichtheim, I, pp. 216–17.
4. *The Prophecies of Neferti*; see Lichtheim, I, pp. 139–45.
5. Breasted, I, 4, 66; 39, 30; 41, 236–7.
6. Lichtheim, I, p. 219.
7. Herodotus, II, p. 152.
8. Ibid., p. 151.
9. Breasted, I, 4, 134, 140 & 146; 41, 98.
10. Hart, 1991, p. 175.

CHAPTER THREE

1. For examples see Lichtheim, I, pp. 83–93.

2. Vandier, 1936.
3. Vandier, 1950.
4. Winlock, 1945.
5. James, 1962.
6. Breasted, II, 439–43; 452–3.
7. For translations of all the works mentioned below see Lichtheim, I.
8. Lichtheim, I, pp. 198–201.
9. Breasted, I, 653–60.
10. Pliny, xxxvi, 13.
11. Josephus, *Against Apion.*
12. In Papyrus Sallier I (British Museum, 10185), dating to Merenptah (1213–1203 BC).
13. Breasted, II, 29–32.
14. Habachi, 1972; excerpts quoted here translated by Watterson.

CHAPTER FOUR

1. Lichtheim, II, p. 12ff.
2. Mentioned in the Bible: Joshua, 19: 6.
3. Breasted, II, 17–25, 344.
4. Breasted, II, 67–73.
5. Breasted, II, 478.
6. Kitchen, 1971.
7. Thutmose III's campaigns are recorded in his Annals,

which are carved on walls in the Temple of Amun at Karnak; see Pritchard, 1969, p. 234ff.

8. Revelations, 16: 16.
9. Recorded in Amenemhab's tomb at Thebes (No. 85).
10. Pritchard, 1969, pp. 247–8.
11. op. cit., p. 244.
12. Moran, 1992.
13. op. cit.
14. Martin, 1991.
15. Published in full, with translations, in 1986, by the Oriental Institute, Chicago, as *The Battle Reliefs of King Sety I.*
16. Percy Bysshe Shelley, 'Ozymandias'.
17. The Turin Judicial Papyrus; see Breasted, IV, 416ff.

CHAPTER FIVE

1. Peet, 1930.
2. Černy, 1975.
3. Edgerton, 1951.
4. Montet, 1942.
5. From the Harris Papyrus 500: translation by Watterson. For examples of love poems see Lichtheim, II, pp. 182–93.

Further Reading

Translations of the classical authors cited in the text are available in the Loeb Classical Library, The World's Classics or Penguin Classics.

Adams, B. *Predynastic Egypt* (Shire Egyptology, 7, 1988)

Adams, B. and Cialowicz, K.M. *Protodynastic Egypt* (Shire Egyptology, 25, 1997)

Aldred, C. *Akhenaten, Pharaoh of Egypt: a New Study* (London, 1968)

Breasted, J.H. *Ancient Records of Egypt* (Chicago, 1906)

Carter, H. *The Tomb of Tutankhamen* (London, 1972)

Černy, J. 'The workmen of the king's tomb', in 'Egypt from the death of Ramesses III to the end of the Twenty-first Dynasty' (Cambridge Ancient History, Vol. II: 2, 1975, Chapter XXXV, pp. 606–75)

Clayton, P. *Chronicle of the Pharaohs* (London, 1994)

David, A.R. *The Pyramid Builders of Ancient Egypt* (London, 1986)

Dodson, A. *Egyptian Rock-cut Tombs* (Shire Egyptology, 14, 1991)

Edgerton, W.F. 'The strikes in Ramses III's twenty-ninth year', *Journal of Near Eastern Studies* (10, 1951, pp. 659–61)

Edwards, I.E.S. *The Pyramids of Egypt* (Penguin Books, 1970)

Emery, W. *Archaic Egypt* (Penguin Books, 1961)

Faulkner, R.O. *The Ancient Egyptian Pyramid Texts* (Oxford, 1969)

Grimal, N. *A History of Ancient Egypt* (Oxford, 1992)

FURTHER READING

Habachi, L. *The Second Stela of Kamose* (Gluckstadt, 1972)

Hart, G. *Pharaohs and Pyramids* (London, 1991)

James, T.G.H. *The Hekanakhte Papers and Other Early Middle Kingdom Documents* (New York, 1962)

Jenkins, N. *The Boat Beneath the Pyramids* (London, 1980)

Kitchen, K.A. *Pharaoh Triumphant: the Life and Times of Ramesses II, King of Egypt* (Warminster, 1982)

——. 'Punt and how to get there', in *Orientalia* (40, 1971, pp. 184–207)

——. *Ramesside Inscriptions, Translated and Annotated – Translations*, I (Oxford, 1993)

——. *The Third Intermediate Period in Egypt* (1100–650 BC) (2nd edn with supplement, Warminster, 1986)

Lauer, J.P. *Saqqara, Royal Cemetery of Memphis* (London, 1976)

Lichtheim, M. *Ancient Egyptian Literature* (vols I–III, Berkeley, 1975–80)

Martin, G.T. *The Hidden Tombs of Memphis* (London, 1991)

Montet, P. *Tanis: douze années de fouilles dans une capitale oublie du Delta Égyptien* (Paris, 1942)

Moran, W.L. *The Amarna Letters* (Baltimore/London, 1992)

Murnane, W.J. *United with Eternity: a Concise Guide to the Monuments of Medinet Habu* (Chicago, 1980)

Peet, T.E. *The Great Tomb-robberies of the Twentieth Egyptian Dynasty* (2 vols, Oxford, 1930)

Pritchard, J.B. (ed.). *Ancient Near Eastern Texts relating to the Old Testament* (3rd edn, Princeton, 1969)

Robins, G. *The Art of Ancient Egypt* (London, 1997)

Romer, J. *Valley of the Kings* (London, 1981)

Spencer, A.J. *Death in Ancient Egypt* (Penguin Books, 1982)

——. *Early Egypt: the Rise of Civilization in the Nile Valley* (London, 1993)

Strouhal, E. *Life in Ancient Egypt* (Cambridge, 1992)

Trigger, B.G. et al, *Ancient Egypt: a Social History* (Cambridge, 1983)

Vandier, J. *La Famine dans l'Égypte Ancienne* (Cairo, 1936)

——. *Mo'alla. La Tombe d'Ankhtifi et la Tombe de Sebekhotep* (Cairo, 1950)

Watson, P. *Egyptian Pyramids and Mastaba Tombs* (Shire Egyptology, 6, 1987)

Watterson, B. *Gods of Ancient Egypt* (Stroud, 1996)

——. *Introducing Egyptian Hieroglyphs* (2nd edn, Edinburgh, 1993)

——. *The Egyptians* (Oxford, 1997)

——. *Women in Ancient Egypt* (Stroud, 1991)

Winlock, H.E. *The Slain Soldiers of Neb-hepet-Re Mentu-hotpe* (New York, 1945)

References to works above are cited below by author and date of publication. Extra references are given in full. The content of several of these works is self-explanatory and needs no amplification.

A complete survey of Egyptological literature is the *Annual Egyptological Bibliography*, which has been published annually since 1947 by the International Association of Egyptologists and the Nederlands Instituut voor het Nabije Oosten, Leiden, and is currently edited by L.M.J. Zonhoven. Each edition contains abstracts of over a thousand books and articles, usually in English no matter what the language of the original.

GENERAL

Grimal (1992) is a political, cultural and economic history of the Egyptians up to their conquest by Alexander the Great; Watterson (1997) covers the same ground and takes the story up to the present day. Clayton (1994) is an account of all the rulers of ancient Egypt in chronological order using timelines and other visual aids.

PREDYNASTIC AND ARCHAIC EGYPT

During the last few years there has been increasing activity in the study of these long-neglected periods of Egyptian history, with new theories on dates and developments. Adams (1988), Adams and Cialowicz (1977) and Spencer (1993) are important but the standard works are Emery (1961) and M. Hoffman, *Egypt Before the Pharaohs*, London, 1979. An excellent brief survey of the period is Trigger's 'The Rise of Egyptian Civilization' in Trigger et al (1983); another is found in Chapter 2 of Watterson (1997).

THE OLD KINGDOM

The classic work on pyramids in general is Edwards (1970) and on the Step Pyramid in particular, Lauer (1976). Hart (1991) is a well-illustrated guide to Old Kingdom pyramids; Jenkins (1980) is the only complete account of Khufu's funerary boat. Watson (1987) is one of the excellent, low cost Shire Egyptology series.

THE MIDDLE KINGDOM

A useful survey of the period is Kemp's 'Old Kingdom, Middle Kingdom and Second Intermediate Period' in Trigger et al (1983). David (1986) is an account of the lives of the workers' who lived in the Twelfth-Dynasty pyramid-workers town at Lahun.

THE NEW KINGDOM

There is much written about the Amarna Period: it is conveniently indexed in G.T. Martin, *A Bibliography of the Amarna Period and its Aftermath: The Reigns of Akhenaten, Smenkara, Tutankhamun and Ay*, London, 1991. Aldred (1968) is a good general survey.

Kitchen (1982) gives an excellent historical survey of the Ramesside Period. The workmen's village at Deir el-Medina is described by Černy (1975).

New Kingdom rock-cut tombs, both royal and private, are briefly described in Dodson (1991); but Romer (1981) is the most informative book on royal tombs of the period at Thebes. Martin (1991) is a well-illustrated account of the Sakkara tombs of General, later King, Horemheb; Maya, Tutankhamun's treasurer; and Tia, sister of Ramesses II.

RELIGION AND SOCIAL LIFE

There is a vast amount of literature of Egyptian religion. A good introduction is S. Quirke, *Ancient Egyptian Religion*, London,

1992. Watterson (1996) is a gazetteer of the most important Egyptian deities and a retelling of the mythological stories connected with them. Spenser (1982) is an easily readable account of ancient Egyptian burials customs.

Strouhal (1992) is a well-illustrated account of the daily lives of ordinary Egyptians from birth to death. Watterson (1991) is an attempt to detail the lives of ancient Egyptian women of all classes.

Index